Common-Sense
church
growth

In honor of
W. Winfred and Elizabeth Moore
whose "work of faith, labor of love, and
steadfastness of hope" have set the benchmark in ministry

Common-Sense
church
growth

Howard K. Batson

SMYTH&HELWYS
PUBLISHING, INCORPORATED · MACON, GEORGIA

Smyth & Helwys Publishing, Inc.
6316 Peake Road
Macon, Georgia 31210-3960
1-800-747-3016
© 1999 by Smyth & Helwys Publishing
All rights reserved.
Printed in the United States of America.

Howard K. Batson

The paper used in this publication meets the minimum
requirements of American National Standard for Information
Sciences—Permanence of Paper for Printed Library Materials.
ANSI Z39.48–1984   (alk. paper)

Library of Congress Cataloging-in-Publication Data

Batson, Howard. K.
    Common-sense church growth
    p. cm.
    1. Church growth.
    2. Christian leadership.
    I. Title.
    BV652.25.B378   1999
    254'.5—dc21   99-14809
                                             CIP
ISBN 1-57312-179-7

The publisher grants permission to the author to forego company policy of using
gender-inclusive language.

Contents

Foreword

It is a privilege and an honor to be asked to write this fore-word. I was for thirty years pastor of First Baptist Church, Amarillo; so I have watched and listened with special interest as this young man, Howard Batson, has pastored, preached to, and led this same church. I am thrilled at the love he demonstrates for the church and his fast involvement in the life of the city. Howie Batson knows who he is. He is self-confident, not egotistical. He has regard for the traditions of a great church and at the same time has shown matchless leadership in changes made and in the making, all for the betterment of everything the church does. For him, the church is not a morgue; neither is it a three-ring circus. He has great respect for the past, but the message and the methods are addressed and geared to the present generation. Howard Batson is and does what he writes.

James F. Byrnes quotes Abraham Lincoln: "If we could first know where we are, and whither we are tending, we could better judge what to do and how to do it." Howard Batson knows where he and his people are and where they are headed. This book will be a road map for many.

Dr. Batson does not mince words. From directions on establishing a healthy pastoral ministry in chapter 1 to treating all church members as valued people in chapter 10, on every page the author writes for our times—times not merely troubled but also stunned and bewildered. He addresses the church's bewilderment and calls our attention to some ways that have been tried to extricate us from our bewilderment that have been far from what Christ called his church to be and to do. Rather than helping, these ways have led to ridicule or into a deeper, dark morass. Like a good lawyer summing up an important case, he calculates the effect of every word as he points to solid, common-sense solutions. If you want to grow a strong, loving church, what do you do in times like these? First, second, third—you may be surprised at the simple, practical list.

Yes, Howie Batson writes what he has done. As I watched him work and listened to his sermons, I was made keenly aware of a new spirit, a return to a positive self-image and a sense of worth and excitement in First Baptist Church, Amarillo.

This book will stand as a testimony that Howard Batson along with the apostle Paul has two magnificent obsessions: "I speak concerning Christ and his church." It is evident that Batson wants to share his joy of discovery in ways that will help ministers and laypersons make their churches greater blessings for Jesus' sake.

I am truly thankful for the writing of this book. There are principles and ideas that should fit and bless all of us. People in the entire Panhandle of Texas already know something about the ethics, work habits, and commitment of Howard Batson. A kindly spirit, dedication to purpose, and high ideals have already been communicated to the people where he lives. It is now important that his ideas and spiritual fervor be put in written form for a much larger audience and for persons yet to come. I heartily commend this book because I truly believe it will be widely read and the principles and ideas put into practice in many places.

—W. Winfred Moore
Director, Center for Ministry Effectiveness
Baylor University

Preface

The church is holy ground. The Spirit moves when and where He wills. Church growth can never be distilled into simple principles, formulas, or platitudes. When God chooses to fulfill the voice of the prophets, our sons and daughters begin to prophesy, and the church begins to dream dreams. As the wind of the Spirit blows where He wills, the church is added to daily.

I would never attempt to encapsulate the Spirit of God or peddle what is holy. We cannot reduce church growth to principles in the same way our colleagues in the business school can delineate the art of marketing under the rubric of "four Ps." Despite this real distinction, the church must never be so mystical that it ignores the practical. Even in the earliest days of the community of faith—as the Spirit was poured forth— matters of poor management threatened to thwart the movement of God's people. Luke explains, "Now at this time while the disciples were increasing in number, a complaint arose" (Acts 6:1). We all remember the "table service dispute" between the Hellenists and the Hebraists. The solution was the enlisting, training, and organizing of seven helpers for a new food distribution system to Grecian widows. In some complex way the uniting of the mystery of the movement of the Spirit with sound management methods has always been a part of effective church growth.

We have all witnessed a congregation in its infancy thrive on one part Spirit and one part enthusiasm. This same congregation, nonetheless, soon discovers it will have to embrace also the "institutional facets" of church that were once deemed as left behind at its traditional sponsoring church. Sooner or later, we have to be pragmatic about managing our churches in a fashion that invites growth.

I will not address spiritual concerns—prayer, fasting, meditation, and seeking the will of God—because I assume these are already taking place both individually in your life and corporately in your community of faith. Leaving these concerns to other writers in other works, this book will focus on pragmatic principles that can assist the movement of the Spirit, as the choosing of the seven assisted the movement of the Spirit in the early church in the Acts of the Apostles.

Three other concerns should be addressed. First, it is imperative that moderate/conservative congregations stop treating church growth as something that should be left to their more fundamentalist brethren. For too long we have ridiculed the questionable methods of church growth that are taking place in fundamentalist congregations without offering any real alternatives. Growing Christ's church as the Kingdom of God is not a fundamentalist agenda—it is the agenda of the Great Commission!

Second, this work is set apart by the fact that it is not trying to address generational tendencies that seem to be the focal point of most church growth manuals. In fact, the words "boomer," "buster," or "Gen-X" seldom appear in the text of this book. For those of you who are weary of the hyperdeleniation between the generations, this should be a welcomed change. For the most part, the principles suggested in this work transcend generational boundaries. Usually, such boundaries are not nearly as evident as most contemporary church growth gurus would have us believe.

Third, this work is written by a pastor who, like many of you, faces the myriad of struggles and demands that are placed upon ministers every day. I have always found it difficult to value the advice given by sociologists, marketers, and pollsters who have never faced the daily struggles in a pastorate. Some "experts" have never actually been the pastor of a growing congregation! More often than not, their advice is idealistic and simplistic. They demonstrate no evidence of comprehending the complex and delicate task of being a pastor. My greatest hope is that many of you with whom I am sharing these ideas will likewise share ideas with me. This book is an invitation to dialogue concerning our most important task, working effectively to reach the world for God's Kingdom. May God bless you in your ministry.

Finally, I must acknowledge my debt to Jan Wood (first reader), Lisa Batson, Hugh Batson, Bill Brian, Nancy Crowley, Bobby Dagnel, Jeff Raines, and Lynda Stafford for proofing the manuscript. All errors, however, remain my own. Their gift of time is greatly appreciated. Also, the project would not be possible without Carol Brian's careful manuscript preparation and research assistance.

I especially want to thank the members of Meadowbrook Baptist Church and First Baptist Church of Amarillo. They have allowed me the privilege of serving as their pastor. Working hand in hand with me as co-laborers for Christ, the members of these churches have employed the principles contained in this book in a faithful manner. I only wish all pastors had the privilege of serving these congregations who love and encourage their pastor, work together in a spirit of unity, and dare to make changes in order to serve more effectively the Kingdom of God.

Establish a healthy pastoral ministry.

A former professional football player took a sales job with an insurance agency. During a sales meeting the manager of the agency began to berate the sales force for a lackluster performance: they weren't meeting projections; they weren't making the calls; and they weren't trying hard enough. The manager said, "Don't make the mistake of thinking you can't be replaced!" He then turned to the former football player and said, "In the NFL when a player didn't meet expectations, they got rid of the player, didn't they?" The football player looked at the sales manager and said slyly, "Actually, if the whole team was doing bad, they would usually get rid of the coach."

Congregations expect a great deal from their pastor. As Rev. Canon Geoffrey Gray concluded,

> People expect their priest to have the skill in sermon composition of Knox, the oratorical power of Churchill, the personal charm of a film star, the tact of royalty, the hide of a hippo, the administrative ability of Lord Nuffield, the wisdom of Socrates, and the patience of Job. Some people must often be disappointed.[1]

Despite the fact that expectations are usually unrealistic, the pastor should be both a leader with great vision and a friend who shares joy and pain. Only rarely will a congregation rise above the vision and expectation of the pastor. Therefore, it is imperative that the pastor lead by word and deed. At the same time, however, he must be perceived as a "real person." People desire a pastor whom "they can talk to." His demeanor must communicate that he cares and is approachable.

Growing churches have a healthy pastoral ministry. Recent months have been particularly difficult for me as I have observed three churches that are very dear to me experience crises surrounding their pastoral ministry. In two cases the pastor has already been forced from his position of leadership. Forced termination of pastors is now a daily occurrence, traumatizing congregations as members take sides against one another. As I have the opportunity to speak with members of pastor search committees, I always inform them that their job is of ultimate importance because nothing will shape the future of a congregation more than the person selected to serve as the pastor.

Lloyd Rediger has made it clear that the greatest asset of a congregation is not its buildings, its programs, or its reputation in the community. The greatest asset is the pastor.[2] The pastor will quite literally "make or break" the congregation. If the congregation selects a pastor with whom they can relate and whom they can respect, then the congregation may see many days of growing and fulfilling ministries. If, on the other hand, the pastor search committee fails to bring a candidate who can relate well to a particular congregation, then the church will face tension, strife, and decline in the days that lie ahead. What should churches look for in a pastor? How can we envision a healthy pastoral ministry?

Serve as a fellow pilgrim.

People want a pastor who is a fellow pilgrim struggling through the challenges and hardships of life. The congregation relates to a pastor who grieves when he finds death visiting his own family, who is disappointed when his own children misbehave, and who has to struggle with sickness and the difficulties of life that everyone must endure. By being a fellow pilgrim, the pastor, like God in Christ, takes on an incarnational approach to ministry. He loves, laughs, cries, and hopes as he experiences life with the members of the congregation.

If the pastor does not relate well to his congregation, his effectiveness will be diminished. For example, take the ministry of David, who has recently accepted his first pastorate. The congregation is composed of farmers and ranchers in the Panhandle of Texas. They are a conservative lot, yet possess the pioneer spirit of West Texas. Being from Washington, D.C., David could not tell the difference between a cow and a bull if he were held at gunpoint! His politics are progressive, and his concerns are from another, younger generation. While he seems a bit oblivious to it, there exists a real barrier that is thwarting the power of his sermons. While his people are accustomed to praying for rain in the worship service, David is more focused in his prayers on human rights and justice. In Washington, D.C., women were a vital part of the deacon body, and David is absolutely shocked at the "backwardness" of his new congregation. It is hard for him to relate to the frankness and openness of his West Texas congregation. More and more, David slips in the back door, puts in his office hours, and quietly goes home.

Friday night high school football is a staple of his new community, yet David's family has never attended, despite many invitations from the locals. His congregation hears more and more about "the way it is back in Washington," and their ears are becoming weary from the phrase. Put bluntly, David is failing to relate to his congregation. Rather than seeing him as a pilgrim or a fellow struggler who understands their hardships and their way of life, they view him as aloof, removed, and condescending.

David has failed to realize that he cannot challenge his congregation to make progress or to move forward until he, himself, has identified with them—right where they are. His family must become part of the community in order to be effective in ministry. His presence at a Friday night football game, cheering on the local team, is just what David needs to do to demonstrate that he has "caught the spirit" of the community.

In many denominations Christians spend a tremendous amount of resources training our ministers for foreign missions. We want to ensure that they can relate to the culture, language, and lifestyle of the indigenous people. Ironically, most denominations fail to realize that a myriad of cultures and communities exists even within the United States. A minister must become one with his community in order to be effective. He can remain the prophet who calls the people to move forward, but only after he has been accepted as a kindred spirit.

What is happening to David, in my estimation, happens to more than half of those who graduate from seminary. They find themselves living as aliens in their communities, failing to identify with the people God has called them to serve. As David senses the congregation withdrawing from him, he is all the more likely to continue to withdraw from them. He does not attend the fiftieth year wedding anniversary of his congregants; he misses Miss Hattie's ninetieth birthday; and he never utters a proud word about the church's city champion softball team. Unless he begins to identify with his community, David will fail to be effective in that congregation.

Are you approachable in ministry? In my first congregation we conducted a ministry effectiveness survey to see how the congregation was relating to the pastor and staff. I'll never forget one of the comments written on the ministry evaluation sheet in the area of pastoral ministry. One of the members at Meadowbrook Baptist Church wrote, "Howie is just not the kind of guy that I could ever share my problems with." I have no reason to think that this person was being vindictive or unfair in his assessment. I ponder to this day what I had done to communicate to that individual that I could not be trusted or be helpful with the challenges found in life. Even though the great majority of the congregation seemed to have no difficulty relating their life issues to me, I was and still am bothered by the critical comment.

Are you approachable? Do you keep confidences in such a way that people know their secrets are safe with you? Do you show a genuine interest in your congregation? Many pastors, through silent signals, make clear to their congregations that they have neither the time nor the interest in pondering the problems of the pilgrims. Memorizing the names, histories, delights, and sorrows of the people will go a long way in fostering church growth.

Develop trust.

In his book, *The Finishing Touch*, Chuck Swindoll shares with his readers a chain letter he received. It reads:

> This chain letter is meant to bring relief and happiness to you. Unlike other chain letters, this does not cost money. Simply send a copy of this letter to six other churches who are tired of their ministers. Then bundle up your pastor and send him to the church at the bottom of the list. In one week you will receive 16,436 ministers—and one of them should be a dandy! One man broke the chain and got his old minister back.[3]

The letter is humorous because it bears much truth. Almost every church member can remember a time when the congregation was trying to rid itself of an incompetent or uncaring pastor.

In order to foster church growth, the congregation and pastor must develop a relationship built on trust. Slowly, a congregation begins to accept the new pastor's leadership, acquire his visions, and capture the burden for ministry he sets before them. The duration of time required for the development of this pastor-people relationship is often influenced by the previous pastor's ministry, for the new pastor inherits the level of trust or distrust established by his predecessor. If a congregation has cause to be suspicious or critical of its previous pastor, the present pastor can be sure their relationship with him will begin with ample caution. If, however, the previous pastor was a shepherd who was faithful to the fold, most members of the congregation will allow the new pastor to inherit the same level of trust until he proves himself unworthy.

The new pastor in the parsonage is to the members of his congregation as a new, young physician is to his patients. Each must prove himself worthy of the trust of his constituents. No one wants to be the first under the scalpel of the novice surgeon. In like fashion, it takes time before members of the congregation will welcome the new pastor to perform their weddings and funerals. As time passes, however, trust builds, and the members welcome the new pastor to celebrate and mourn the stages of life with them. It is foolish for a new pastor to feel anxious, jealous, or threatened as the church continues to invite its previous pastor to preside over important occasions. Just as patients want to go to a physician they know and trust, congregations have a natural desire to continue to place their trust in proven hands. In fact, a confident pastor can see a deep and abiding relationship between the previous pastor and the people as a sign that he, too, will have an opportunity over the years to build such a rapport with the people. Over time, as one serves as a faithful pastor, trust builds.

Interpersonal Skills. Speed Leas, often described as one of the world's foremost authorities on church conflict, concluded that the primary cause of church conflicts is a pastor's lack of interpersonal competence. This symptom usually takes shape on different poles. At one end, some clergy are withdrawn and apathetic, lacking initiative and failing to provide leadership. At the other, pastors are contentious and authoritarian.[4]

The result often starts out as a normal deacon's meeting. Then someone clears his throat and says, "Ah, pastor, while you were on vacation, some of us had a meeting. Some people are saying they're not getting fed spiritually. Our church finances are down. Our attendance isn't what it should be. We feel some changes need to be made. Pastor, we—ah—feel we need a change in the pulpit. We'd like for you to look for another church and be out of the parsonage in no more than three months."[5] Southern Baptist pastors are being terminated at a rate of 116 per month or one every six hours.[6] In the climate of forced terminations, pastors can gain the trust of their congregations if they demonstrate excellent communication skills. If you are a pastor, ask yourself these questions:

• Am I even-tempered and positive in my demeanor?
• Do I try to avoid using the pulpit as a weapon in congregational battles?
• Do I promptly and appropriately return phone calls, answer letters, and follow through with promises made while passing in the hallway?
• Am I careful to treat all members of the congregation fairly and equally, never showing partiality?
• Do I distribute my time evenly among the various generationas?
• Am I careful not to speak negatively of one church member to another church member?
• Do people feel valued when they encounter me in conversation?
• Am I too busy talking about "me, myself, and I?"

Nothing is more important to the success of a pastor than demonstrating strong interpersonal skills. Treating people as you prefer to be treated is the first step toward building a relationship of trust with your congregation.

Sensitivity. Pastors who succeed are those who have mastered the gift of listening more and talking less. Arriving in the parsonage with a narrow agenda that discounts the particular needs of your community of faith will prove disastrous for your ministry.

Peter had been called to serve the Shady Grove Evangelical Church. He and his wife, Sandi, had dreamed of receiving the finest Christian education for their daughter, Tiffany. While Peter had not mentioned his desire to the pastor search committee, he did privately ponder how Shady Grove's Sunday School rooms could double as classrooms for his dream, the "Dayspring Christian School."

If Peter had taken the time to listen to his congregation, he would have learned that many of the local educators—both administrators and teachers—attended Shady Grove. They were honored annually for their commitment to the community during the church's Educator's Appreciation Day. On this day the pastor traditionally showered the public school system with accolades. By pursuing his personal dream at Shady Grove, Peter will make the fatal mistake of acting before listening.

The art of listening to a congregation is especially difficult because divergent groups within the congregation send different signals. A progressive party may be pushing the pastor to ordain women as deacons for the first time in the history of the fellowship, while the fundamentalist faction cannot ponder such a possibility. The younger adults may make known their desire for praise choruses on a projection screen and the rhythm of a guitar, while seniors revere the traditional hymnal and the dignity of a pipe organ.

Despite these mixed messages, the pastor must find the central voice of the people while appreciating and acknowledging all minority voices. I am impressed with Eric Holleyman, my successor at Meadowbrook Baptist Church. When Eric Holleyman began his ministry at Meadowbrook, he took the first few weeks to listen to the congregation rather than charging in with his own agenda. Thoughtfully and carefully, he met with small groups within the congregation and invited members to respond on index cards as he interviewed them concerning their hopes and fears. They had an opportunity to share with their new pastor what they felt had worked well in the past and what they deemed to have been insufficient. Sitting down with the people in the first few days and taking the time to listen and record their voices was a masterful way for Eric to work through the thoughts of a medium-sized congregation. Things continue to go well for him at Meadowbrook because the congregation knows that their pastor is "all ears." In listening to the divergent voices, a pastor will discover the history, ministry goals, and real needs of the congregation.

Preparation. People trust a pastor who plans carefully and thoughtfully. As a pastor and committee present proposals to the congregation for affirmation, the pastor must prove knowledgeable about the concerns of the members. No question should arise from the floor that the pastor and committee have not already considered and prepared to answer honestly and openly.

Have you heard the parable of the truck driver who tried to squeeze under an overpass that was one-half inch too low? Traffic was stalled for miles, and the city called out all of its engineers to contemplate how to remove the wedged truck trailer from beneath the overpass. A young lad was hushed as he constantly tried to gain the attention of the city's chief engineer, who was pondering the alternative solutions to the dilemma. After many hours of study and traffic congestion, the chief engineer decided cranes would be needed to lift the prestressed concrete beams three quarters of an inch so the driver could back the trailer out from its wedged state. Because of the boy's persistence, however, the city engineer finally turned to the young boy and said, "Now tell me, son, what is it that you want? Can't you see I'm busy?" The little boy replied, "Well, all I wanted to say was if you let a little air out of his tires, he'll squeeze right through!"

Like the city engineer, the pastor must not be so busy contemplating complex solutions that he loses the ability to see the situation through the eyes of common wisdom. "Just let the air out of the tires" is sometimes the best response from the floor of a church business meeting. Concerns become fewer and fewer with each proposal as the people begin to trust their pastor as he works with committees. They realize, once again, that their pastor and committees have "done their homework."

Preach with integrity.

Preaching is a very important ingredient for church growth. As prospective church members visit from congregation to congregation, they intuitively compare sermon to sermon and proclaimer to proclaimer. Far too many pastors serve leftovers hastily thrown together on Saturday evening. Inevitably, our lack of preparation is evident to everyone but ourselves. Fred Craddock, during the Distinguished Preachers Series at Baylor University in 1997, declared, "Whoever does not study has broken the first and great commandment: to love the Lord thy God with all of your heart, soul, mind, and strength." According to the book of Galatians, even Paul was accused of preaching the sermons of Jerusalem, the sermons of the other apostles. Paul vehemently denied this. Preach from your own experience.[7]

In order for sermons to be effective, preparation should include solid biblical exegesis, contemporary illustrations, creative design and delivery, and practical application. Variety should be a foremost goal of every sermon repertoire. Some sermons should encourage; others should challenge. Some should rebuke; others should teach. Are your sermons targeted at different generations? Are your illustrations applicable to the various demographic groups within your community of faith?

Because we want the congregation to be able to apply on Monday what they have heard on Sunday, the temptation for the contemporary pulpiteer is to exchange expository proclamation for pop psychology. Biblical themes of sin, Savior, forgiveness, charity, hope, and healing are exchanged for "points for parenting" or "success without stress." Faithful proclamation will not allow the preacher to abandon the great motifs of Scripture for topics that sound more like a talk radio show than the theology of the apostles.

Surprisingly, as we explore much of the church growth material available today, we find that one of the central themes is that worship services ought to be designed for "seekers." Recently I received a flyer in the mail that introduced me to a new congregation in Amarillo that promised to provide a very positive experience. The brochure declared that I would "not even have to endure a sermon," because the pastor/speaker simply shared life application stories dealing with "addiction, anger, happiness, and relationships."[8] The brochure also promised that the worship service would be brief. The one-hour-and-fifteen-minute guarantee sounded to me more like an oil change than worship! The pamphlet boasted that I would not be asked for money. Throughout it reflected many of the themes stressed in the voluminous church growth materials designed to help churches reach out to their communities.

The advice can often be distilled to the message: "If you do not challenge, offend, confront, or exclude, then the masses will come and worship with you." This compromised church growth allows the worshiper, rather than the one worshiped, to determine what is acceptable and what is not acceptable in the act of worship. Such culturally baptized methodologies are void of the awe every sinner experiences when he finds himself in the presence of a Holy God. Such casual gatherings, in unthreatening circumstances, fail to join with the prophet Isaiah as he declares, "Woe is me, for I am a man of unclean lips among a people of unclean lips" (Isa 6:5). While the intentions of contemporary evangelicals are pure, they literally threaten the basic theology of worship.

While the themes we preach are nonnegotiables, the style and type of delivery are open avenues. The "three points and a poem" methodology can be exchanged for dramatic monologues or storytelling. Often the mode can be fluid even if the message is fixed. Preaching with integrity allows the method to vary but demands that the message remain the same. We must be careful, however, never to compromise the message even if doing so might stimulate temporary growth.

Communicate care.

The pastor's ministry serves as a model of caring. Growing churches lead their members to become a caring family, ministering to one another. A couple recently moved to the city of Amarillo from a nearby smaller town. We learned that the husband was going to have major surgery the next week. They were without local church support and were in real need of ministry. We sent someone to the hospital every day to pray and visit with this dear couple. We never mentioned that we were desirous of their church membership; we simply shared the love and care of Christ. Immediately, upon the husband's recovery from surgery, the couple became members of our congregation. They even expressed their gratitude for the fact that while making hospital visits, no one ever asked them to join. Rather, we were exhibiting a caring spirit. Just as this couple was drawn into our church, the community is drawn to the church when it sees a loving, ministering congregation.

Fast-growing congregations will not be able to sustain their momentum if they do not also strive to meet the needs of those who have already become members of the church.

Have you ever heard of the "back door problem?" I once was a member of a congregation where, Sunday after Sunday, the aisles were filled with people coming forward for membership. This seemed thrilling until I realized that the actual number of people in the pews was not increasing. Finally I realized that just as many people were going out the "back door" as were coming in the "front door." Unless new members are assimilated by receiving and giving ministry, their attendance will be haphazard. Church growth becomes something like a mirage in the desert; it seems real but vanishes when actually put to the test. One congregation in Texas baptized more than 1,700 persons during the last five years, only to, surprisingly, witness average attendance in church Bible study decline by 434 persons.[9] Where did the people go? Out the back door! A comprehensive pastoral care program ministers to the entire congregation, making every member a vital part of the church body.

Be a faithful steward.

The church's business affairs and the administration of its various programs must be overseen with the greatest of care. The church is God's business. Budgets, loans, and personnel policies should reflect the very best tools and philosophies available.

While it may be unfortunate, the pastor will spend more time on administrating than he does on any other single task, regardless of the size of the congregation. Successful administration keeps programs and projects moving in a progressive direction. The church members will expect the church to be managed by the same professional standards they encounter in the very best companies.[10] The church must have clear, updated personnel policies, a working committee structure, and policies dealing with everything from weddings and funerals to kitchen management.

Even many medium-sized churches attempt to combine food service, classroom education, library science, recreation programming, choral performance, property management, drama lessons, and daycare into a single institution. This collection of entities can quickly become a management nightmare if not properly overseen. The pastor, staff, and committees must form a team that is able to address every need from government guidelines for food preparation and sanitation to sexual misconduct insurance for child-care workers. Successful administration requires strong pastoral leadership.

At the same time, administrative decisions should be marked by open and honest communication, ensuring that people never feel as if they have no voice in the business affairs of the church. The congregation wants to be informed and involved in the process of making major decisions. Even the strongest form of pastoral leadership must include the laity in the administration of church affairs if the process is to embody the integrity and openness that should characterize church management.

Have a healthy outlook.

One of the greatest ecclesiastical myths is that the minister must please all the church members all of the time. If any minister were ever able to accomplish this goal, he would have to exceed the abilities of Christ and the apostles (especially Paul), who experienced difficulties in ministry.

According to a recent report, pressures are increasing for pastors, thereby creating a crisis in many churches of various denominations. Stress mounts for pastors as they deal with unrealistic expectations, pressures on their families, transitions to new styles of worship, financial difficulties, and isolation. Eventually, problems for the pastor lead to problems for the church.

Ike Patterson removed himself from the ministry several years ago because of stress. He remembers,

> People want pastors now who are young, who know every organizational skill, who are able to preach as good as any of the [preachers of] larger churches on television and at the same time can bandage up scraped knees, come eat supper with them, and go to every meeting of every ladies' or men's prayer group in the church.[11]

Patterson said that the changes in his denomination and unrealistic expectations from his nearly 700 "bosses," or church members, led to burnout. His twenty-four-hour-a-day job was taking its toll on his family.

Perhaps you've heard the story of the mother who frantically tried to awaken her son: "Get up, son. Today is Sunday. Sunday School begins at 9:30." "I know, Mother, but I'm not going today." "Why not?" she inquired. "I'll give you two reasons," he replied. "First, I don't feel like getting up this morning. Second, no one down at the church likes me. Everybody is against me." Insistently, the mother continued, "But son you've got to get out of bed, and I'll give you two reasons to do so. First, you're 29 years old. Second, you're the pastor of the church!"[12]

Any pastor who tries to please everyone will soon weary himself. What makes one generation happy will very likely make the next generation angry. Father Joseph Greer once said,

You have to be nuts to go into ministry. It's an awful job. The pay is terrible. The hours are worse. People not only do not look up to you. They look down. You have to love God, and if you don't, it will grind you up. Remember, no trumpets will sound. And you are going to spend more time being a carpenter than a minister.[13]

Ministry is hard enough without focusing on a few negative persons. Did you hear the story about the pastor who was called to a church with 107 positive votes and three negative votes? Instead of rejoicing over his overwhelming landslide, the pastor set out to change the mind of the three negative voters. Two years later, another vote was taken. This time the pastor was removed from the congregation. The vote? Three for and 107 against. This fictitious story illustrates a good point. Many pastors spend entirely too much time trying to please those who refuse to cooperate with their community of faith.

Jean Culli, a pastor's wife, remembers:

In the early days of our ministry I thought if I worked hard enough in the church I would avoid all criticism. What I actually did was provide a bigger bullseye for target practice. I even thought I could stop people from criticizing the pastor to me by declaring: "Please don't tell me your complaints. I never pass them along. You need to talk to him yourself." . . . In our present pastorate, sometime after the honeymoon stage had worn off but before we began to dream of running away, a "friend" came to me and said "someone else" (Do your churches have a lot of "someone elses"? Ours is just full of them.) had said I didn't look "happy to be there anymore." I thought it was sufficient to curb my tongue. Now I have to look happy when I do it. So I simply had smile electrodes surgically implanted in my cheeks. They're automatically activated by an electric current emanating from the front door of our church. But it's just a matter of time until someone tells me I don't look sad enough when they're telling me of some awful happening in their family, and I happen to be close to the church door.[14]

As Jean Culli realized, criticism is an unavoidable part of ministry. Paul was criticized; Jesus was criticized; and every other minister of the gospel has been criticized. While being a people-pleaser can be a very advantageous attribute for a pastor, in its uncontrolled form, it leads to misplaced priorities and stress. Pastors of growing churches must remember not to dwell on the few members of the congregation who have always been, and always will be, negative.

Put family first.

Being on call twenty-four hours a day, seven days a week causes strain in a pastor's relationship with his own family. No church ultimately benefits when the pastor's relationship with his wife and children is sacrificed—even for the sake of the work of God's Kingdom. The deacons and/or personnel committee must take an active role in demanding that the congregation allow the pastor to spend time with his family.

There was once a little boy whose father was the pastor of the nearby Baptist church. The family was eating dinner one evening, and the father, dressed in his suit and gulping down his food, was obviously in a hurry to leave. The boy looked at his dad and asked,

"Daddy, are you going somewhere tonight?"

"Yes, son," he replied, "I am going visiting."

"What is visiting?" the little fellow asked.

"Well," the father began, "visiting is when people from the church go out together into the community to meet people. They pray with them, talk for a while, tell them about Jesus, and just get to know them as friends."

The little boy grew silent for a few minutes and then thought out loud, "Boy, I wish someone would come and visit us!" The father, who had been spending a great deal of time away from home because of the demands of the church, realized what his son meant.

The dad did leave. Fifteen minutes later the doorbell rang. The little boy answered the door and discovered his father standing on the porch.

"Hello," his dad said, "I am the pastor of the church next door, and I have come to visit with you and your family tonight."

So they told Bible stories and prayed. They played games and ate snacks. They spent time getting to know each other.

Churches that are growing demand more of a pastor's time than churches that are plateaued. While the pastor should do everything possible to reach more people for the Kingdom of God, he must never do so at the expense of sacrificing his family on the altar of evangelism.

Conclusion

Churches without a healthy pastoral ministry will seldom, if ever, grow. An effective pastoral ministry will include identifying with the community, developing trust, casting a vision, preaching with integrity, ministering with care, administrating with excellence, managing criticism, and prioritizing family. Obviously, it is almost impossible for any one minister to excel in all of these areas. Selecting a staff that complements the pastor's strengths and weaknesses allows for the formulation of an outstanding team—the focus of the next chapter.

Notes

[1]Canon Geoffrey Gray, "Points to Ponder," *Reader's Digest* (September 1989) 197. As a pastor, Thom Rainer surveyed his deacons to establish their collective, minimum expectations. The result was a 114-hour work week including prayer (14 hours), sermon preparation (18 hours), outreach visitation (10 hours), counseling (10 hours), hospital and home visitation (15 hours), administrative functions (18 hours), community involvement (5 hours), denominational involvement (5 hours), church meetings (5 hours), and worship services/preaching (10 hours). Thom S. Rainer, *Giant Awakenings* (Nashville: Broadman and Holman Publishing, 1995) 109-10.

[2]Lloyd Rediger, "Triage for Wounded Clergy," *Christian Ministry* 26/6 (November/December 1995): 11-12.

[3]Charles Swindoll, *The Finishing Touch* (Dallas: Word Publishing, 1994) 559.

[4]Kevin Miller and Marshall Shelley, "Inside Church Fights: An Interview with Speed Leas," *Leadership* (Winter 1989): 12-20.

[5]Roy C. Price, "When the Pastor Gets Fired," *Leadership* (Fall 1983): 51.

[6]"Forced Termination Survey" (Nashville: Baptist Sunday School Board of the Southern Baptist Convention, 1988) 1-4, unpublished. For more recent studies, see Charles Willis, "Survey: Fewer Pastors Being Fired," *Baptist Standard* 110/38 (23 September 1998): 1, which reported that 892 pastors were involuntarily terminated in 1997 in Southern Baptist churches. Many more terminations, however, are never reported as such. Robert O'Brien, "When Ministers Are Forced Out, Ministry Group Is Ready To Step In," *Fellowship* 8/6 (July/August 1998): 16-17; and David L. Goetz, "Forced Out," *Leadership* (Winter 1996): 40-54.

[7]Fred Craddock, "The Preacher and Preaching," 1997 Baylor University Ministers Conference, Waco TX, 14-15 April 1997.

[8]To protect a congregation that had good intentions, a citation will not be given.

[9]Baptist General Convention of Texas Annuals, 1992, 1993, 1994, 1995, 1996. For obvious reasons, the congregation will remain nameless.

[10]Our staff is currently reading *Customers for Life* by Carl Sewell and Paul B. Brown (New York: Pocket Books, 1990). This is a good example of a secular work that can teach the pastor and staff solid management principles. We discuss each chapter as a group.

[11]Ellen Dockham, "Clergy Stress Called a Crisis for Churches," *Greenville News* (Greenville SC), 20 March 1994, B1.

[12] *Young Adult Bible Study Quarterly* (Nashville: Baptist Sunday School Board of the Southern Baptist Convention) 21 July 1991, 22.

[13] Father Joseph Greer, *Current Thoughts and Trends* (December 1994): 15.

[14] Jean Culli, "Fables of the Pastorate," *Proclaim* (January-March 1996): 8.

Build an exemplary staff.

Church growth flows from an exemplary staff. Unfortunately, churches often attract personnel who are seeking refuge from challenging, secular employment. These individuals fail to recognize that church work can be the most demanding work. In fact, at First Baptist Church of Amarillo, our full-time ministers are fortunate when they have the opportunity to work only sixty hours a week. Not only must ministerial staff be dedicated to work during the day, but also their evenings are filled with activities such as committee meetings, outreach visits, Wednesday evening activities, Sunday School parties, and weekend retreats—not to mention fourteen hours on Sunday. Ministry is a task that is never completed, and, thus, there are always papers on the desk, visits to be made, and programs to be planned and implemented. Every church staff member must be a model of commitment, integrity, and hard work. Their ministry must be a calling and not simply a "job" if they want to endure the inevitable long hours, disappointments, and criticisms that accompany ministry.[1]

The church staff will determine the future of the congregation. A pastor who is not undergirded by a capable staff is much like a quarterback who has no offensive line to block, no receivers to catch, and no running backs to rush. He will soon find himself very unsuccessful in his attempt to gain yardage. The ministers must not only be individually competent, but also able to come together and form a separate community within the community of faith.

It is astonishing that some pastors invest so little time and energy in the selection and design of their ministry team. Any pastor who has tried to rid himself of an incompetent or misplaced staff member knows that hiring the wrong person for the position is unfair to the ministry team, the congregation, and the staff member himself. Poor hiring creates an atmosphere of tension, frustration, disappointment, and trauma on the part of both the pastor and the staff member. In the haste to "fill a position," pastors make poor decisions without conducting a thorough search before selecting a staff member. First Baptist Church of Amarillo recently spent more than twenty-four months in search of a minister to singles. There were numerous times we simply could have "made a hire," but just the right person who would complement our existing ministry team had not been discovered. It is always good to remember that the same church members who push you into a "quick hire" are the first ones to harp and complain should you hire someone who is less than successful in his new staff position.

The pastor and search committee are often able to earn the time necessary to conduct a thorough investigation and search by informing the appropriate church members that, indeed, the absence of a staff member is in no way due to lack of effort on the part of the pastor and committee. In our case, the minister of education informed the singles council on a monthly basis as to what steps we had taken and how many candidates had been interviewed during that period. Because the leaders within the singles division were aware of our efforts, they were patient with the process.

Seek successful employees.

Gather names. The process for seeking a staff member begins by gathering many appropriate names from many diverse sources. Writing to seminaries, inquiring at universities, and calling upon colleagues and other successful ministers serving in similar positions in other congregations are all valuable sources for obtaining résumés. Even in this beginning stage the pastor and search committee should bathe the entire process with prayer. The pastor, the congregation, and the potential staff minister all want God's hand at work in the mysterious process. Looking for God's hand in the process, however, does not excuse the pastor or committee from doing their tasks to ensure an appropriate hire. This work begins with a list of possible candidates.

Play private investigator. As résumés of potential candidates are gathered, the pastor and committee need to make reference checks. A thorough job of reference-checking involves much more than simply calling the names listed on the résumé. As I make reference checks, those individuals simply serve as a source for other names, who serve as a source for other names, who serve as a source for other names. By the end of an exhaustive investigation, I am three or four times removed from the original names given to me by the candidate himself.[2]

During the process of checking references it is of utmost importance that the inquirer not lead the reference. Do not ask questions in such a way that you will simply confirm what you have presupposed. For example, I never ask a question assuming I am going to get a favorable response. I once received a phone call from a church that was considering hiring an acquaintance of mine for a staff position. I made every attempt to give the inquirer an honest evaluation of the candidate's strengths and weaknesses.[3] I accentuated the candidate's positive attributes while giving a few hints as to what the potential employer might want to investigate further. During the course of the conversation the committee member refused to receive any negative signals from me. In fact, on my second attempt, he actually corrected me, insisting that what I said could not possibly hold any merit. This committee member did not want an honest evaluation; he wanted to receive affirmation of his own foregone conclusions. Unlike this prejudiced inquirer, state your questions in such a way that not only allows your reference to be negative, but also continues to probe at any hints of the candidate's weaknesses.

Without exception, every person leaves a track record. Ours is a task of discovering that pattern or record of performance. Rather than being persuaded by a single negative reference or a solitary positive reference, the pastor or committee member should be busy putting together the "candidate's puzzle." If pieced properly, the end result will be a composite of the candidate's strengths and weaknesses. For example, if the educational minister you are considering works very well with senior adults but fails to relate to single adults, then an exhaustive investigation should reveal this strength and this weakness. As you continue to make your reference checks, you will be pleased that you are hearing the same information shared over and over again. Then, with some confidence, you can be assured that you have completed a reliable background check.

For a completely thorough investigation, locate church leaders within a congregation that has previously been served by your candidate, and candidly ask those lay leaders if they would hire that candidate again if they were in a position to do so. Personalizing the context and placing them in your position as the decision-maker often brings the issue home, allowing the reference to be more candid. Of course, all care should be taken to make sure the inquiry does not threaten the candidate's present place of service. I always have a verbal contract of confidentiality before I proceed to ask questions.

A thorough investigation includes doing all the necessary research beyond reference checks. Credit checks, while sometimes overlooked, may yield vital information. Almost as an afterthought, I performed a credit check on a staff candidate just before he was hired at First Baptist Church. He was a talented individual; all of his reference checks were stellar; and his past performance had been outstanding. The credit check, however, revealed he had more than $100,000 in credit card debt! Upon receiving this information, the search committee decided not to become involved with this individual whose daily life would be burdened with overwhelming financial stress.[4]

Transcripts from educational institutions the candidate attended should be gathered by the committee. It is not unheard of for a pastor or staff member to claim to have attended a college or seminary when, in fact, the educational institution has no record of his ever being enrolled. Transcripts can be obtained by having the candidate sign a release and should be mailed directly from the educational institution to the pastor or committee.

If applicable, the spouses of potential staff members should be a part of the interview process. If a spouse will not be happy living in your community, then you can be sure the staff member will be miserable, too. No later than the second or third interview, the spouse should be questioned to make sure he or she also feels the call to serve your congregation.

Avoid faulty logic. Do not assume that a decline within the candidate's current congregation is a sure indication that his ministry with your congregation will yield the same poor results. For example, I once hired a staff member who was in a declining congregation. My investigation revealed that the decline was in no way related to this particular staff member. Even Barry Sanders, arguably the best running back ever to play in the National Football League, would appear to be a very poor running back if he had to follow a lackluster offensive line.

Conversely, do not assume that growth in the candidate's current or previous congregations assures future growth in your community of faith. Your candidate may, for example, be serving in a geographical area of explosive population growth where church growth is more dependent upon location than a staff member's gifts. While I know absolutely nothing about basketball—I only played in a children's church league and was so inept that both sides cheered when I made a point—even I could have coached the 1992 Olympic Dream Team to victory. The fact that the coach, Chuck Daly, was able to win a gold medal in this particular instance tells us very little about his coaching abilities. Be careful not to make simplistic conclusions based upon correlations that have nothing to do with cause and effect.

Treat candidates fairly. The church should treat potential employees as professionals. As a minimum standard, the church must make every effort to reimburse candidates for expenses incurred during the hiring process. Also, churches are notorious for failing to keep potential employees informed. On many occasions potential staff members send résumés to churches and never receive even a simple acknowledgment. This is unfair and thoughtless treatment of anxious candidates.

The pastor and committee should be completely honest with the candidate in regard to the challenges and difficulties that lie ahead. Promises should not be made that cannot be kept. For example, calling a minister to serve in the dual position of minister to preschoolers and children under the impression that the combination is only temporary is unacceptable unless a church has specific goals and plans for making the promise a reality by dividing the position. Honesty also includes clearly communicating what will be expected of the employee. For one potential employee, I actually created a mock schedule depicting an average week on the job. I included normal working hours, church activities, committee meetings, emergency calls, weddings, and funerals as part of this hypothetical schedule. Therefore, we both were assured there would be no surprises when he began his tasks. He could see from the beginning that his work week was going to amount to approximately sixty hours. To ensure a clear meeting of the minds, all arrangements, including vacation days, sick days, insurance, and other benefits, should be communicated explicitly in writing.

Understand the staff's impact. The church's success or failure will often depend on the talent and commitment of its staff. Successful ministry is dependent upon successful programs; successful programs are dependent upon a successful staff. A pastor will soon find that no matter how stimulating and insightful his sermons might be, no one person can build a church in today's culture. Unfortunately, families "shop" for a church today, looking for the best programs. Singles look for singles' activities; young families look for a strong preschool and children's department; middle-aged families with teens look for a dynamic youth ministry; and musicians look for a strong choral program.

As I visit prospective families, I am surprised by the very candid list of programs they are seeking in a church: "Does your church have Bible drill for children?" "Our last church had a very strong handbell choir. Does your church have a good handbell choir?" The "church shopper" sees programs as options, like a compact disc player or leather seats on a car. I am very fortunate to have strong staff and can honestly and confidently inform potential church members that we have everything they could possibly be looking for in preschool care, children's programming, youth activities, singles ministry, senior adult activities, music ministry, and missions involvement. There have been times in my ministry when I struggled to be enthusiastic about the programs in a particular area, often because the staff member in that area was not meeting the needs of his subcongregation.

Dynamic preaching makes for a great pep rally but soon wears thin as families look for depth in a church's ministry. For example, when I went to Meadowbrook Baptist Church, just a few miles away from the campus of Baylor University, I supposed that my youthfulness (I was twenty-eight years old) and enthusiasm would attract the university students to the

27

church. Besides, I was a fellow "Baylor Bear" myself. To my surprise, I found that, even after serving in the church for two years, we still had only eight people in our university department—the same number we had when I began. Finally, in my third year at Meadowbrook, James and Terri Tippit and Steven and Susan Blaschke volunteered to work with our students. The Tippits and Blaschkes were young, energetic couples who were employed by Baylor. Within six months our college department grew from eight students to eighty. The preaching and music had remained constant, but the difference was in programming support.

Form a team.

Because a church staff is much more than a simple gathering of talented individuals, they should never appear to be an all-star team so packed with attention-grabbing superstars that they fail to function collectively. Before calling a new staff member, you have to ponder: Will she complement our present staff? Can we envision her at a staff meeting, giving healthy input into the church's ministry?

The pastor must be very careful not to create a sense of competition among his staff. When one staff member enjoys a successful ministry event or program, the entire staff should be able to rejoice together. A staff member who is not a team player never grasps the vision of the pastor for the congregation. He is much like the selfish basketball star who takes a shot every time he touches the ball. He refuses to listen to the game plan. He stays on the court, raises his hands, and shouts, "Give *me* the ball!" Our present ministry team certainly has moments of disagreement, and we often debate behind closed doors. When we leave a staff meeting, however, we are all "on the same page" and operating with the "same game plan," supporting each other much like a family. While we might bicker among ourselves, we will not tolerate church members berating another staff member, for in doing so, they have criticized our entire team.

Staff members who are incompetent bring the pastor more headaches than help. Veteran pastors have often expended much energy and effort putting out the fires their "helpers" have created. As Dr. Winfred Moore, pastor emeritus of First Baptist Church of Amarillo, has been overheard saying, "It takes a real good education minister to beat none!" There is much truth to Dr. Moore's adage. No staff member is much better than an incompetent staff member. Therefore, it is completely puzzling to me why some pastors, consciously or unconsciously, hire weak team players. It is almost as if they are intimidated by staff members who might be successful. Could we, as pastors, possibly have a fear of sharing the spotlight?

Instead of being threatened by staff members whom the congregation praises, the pastor should glow in their successes because the staff is an extension of his own ministry. When our staff is doing well, I am doing well. When the parents of our teenagers are happy, I am happy. I try to seize every opportunity to publicly praise our staff members. For example, in recent days I have used my pastor's column in our weekly newsletter to report the successes of our staff. Also, on Sunday evenings we have a "word of testimony with the pastor." During this time I interview staff members, publicly praising them and their ministry. The congregation begins to feel good about their ministry team when they see the staff members thriving under the leadership and authority of the pastor.

The staff members also know that as they are loyal to me, the loyalty will be reciprocated. If a church member wants to attack a staff member, then she must come through me first! If the staff members operate in accordance with our agreed-upon team plan, then the church member is not unhappy with the staff member—he is unhappy with me. I will take the blame for the failures of a team member. Put bluntly, when things are going well, praise your staff; when things are not going well, absorb the blame. The staff will learn to function under your supervision and protection and feel much more at home under your leadership. They realize very quickly that you have not abandoned them or left them unprotected from the congregation.

Growing churches have staff members who are involved in outreach. When the pastor takes the initiative and sets the pace, the staff will soon join in the effort to reach out to new families. I often tell our staff that they should each have families they are "working with" in regard to evangelism and church membership. When I know a family is looking for a particular program, I will often send the appropriate programming minister out to meet them and to discuss what our church is doing in their area of interest. I unapologetically ask the staff member to report back to me after having successfully completed the contact. There is no doubt in our ministers' minds that outreach is serious business!

Strive for excellence.

Milton Cunningham, chaplain at Baylor University, says there are two really hard things to find in life: a good spouse and good staff members. They are both important to your well-being. How do you know when a candidate will make a great staff member? During a recent staff retreat I challenged our staff to strive to fit the description of thirteen adjectival categories. If we find someone who can be described by these adjectives, we have found an outstanding staff member.

Loyal. A staff member must be loyal to the pastor, the staff team, and the congregation. Those who are opportunity-seekers rather than loyalists will never give the pastor the support he needs to serve the congregation well. The pastor and other staff members should never have to look for daggers behind their backs.

Timely, Accurate, Dependable. Allegheny Community College offered a free course to senior citizens entitled "How To Improve Your Memory." The instructor was supposed to arrive a half hour before the nine o'clock program was to begin. A student remarked, "When we didn't see him by 8:50, we called his house. He had forgotten!"[5]

Achieving success within the community and earning respect from community professionals depend upon our being timely, accurate, and dependable. Staff members must return all phone calls, answer all letters, and accomplish all tasks in a timely manner. Timeliness shows a respect for other people. Accuracy demonstrates that a staff member is not satisfied with less than excellence. Dependability enhances trust and confidence in the team member. A congregation and pastor soon lose respect for staff members who are undependable, tardy, and sloppy.

Appreciative, Encouraging, Supportive, Sensitive. The most powerful words in all the English language are "thank you." At the height of his popularity Rudyard Kipling was one of the most widely read authors of all time. At one point it was estimated that each word he had in print was worth twenty-five shillings. The story circulates that a group of students at Oxford University pooled their change and sent twenty-five shillings to Kipling. Their accompanying letter read, "Send us your best word." Before long, the reply came. With great anticipation, the students opened the envelope from Kipling to find a single word printed on the piece of paper, "Thanks."[6] Staff members who communicate their appreciation to lay leadership will find themselves with eager and enthusiastic volunteers. Everyone wants to feel appreciated for volunteering his time, expertise, and energies to the church. The staff member who does not write thank-you notes every day is probably falling behind in the category of being appreciative.

An encouraging staff member acts as a catalyst to raise volunteer leaders to the next level of excellence. Supportive staff members enable church volunteers to know that they are not "out on a limb" alone. The staff member is willing to provide the expertise and materials necessary to allow the volunteer to do her job in a rewarding fashion. Sensitive staff members are aware of the personal issues and struggles that might be affecting the performance and commitment of their volunteers.

Motivating, Challenging, Visionary. The children's ministry will never exceed the visions and challenges of the children's minister. While the staff member must be realistic, he should always urge the volunteers to seek more efficient ways of serving. A staff member of excellence is always looking at better and more effective—not easier—ways of doing ministry. By conversing with her peers, a staff member can discover what is working in other communities of faith and tailor these methods to fit her own setting.

Flexible, Consistent. Any staff member who is so rigid as to appear inflexible will be perceived by the congregation as being insensitive. At the same time, however, the staff member's instructions, expectations, and behavioral patterns must be viewed as consistent. Inconsistency breeds uncertainty, and uncertainty breeds a lack of trust.

Confident, Humble. A staff member must not be easily intimidated by church members. Being confident means that he is not easily threatened by others. In every congregation there are a few lay leaders who perceive themselves as the sole decision-makers of the community of faith. Perhaps they are CEOs in the workplace and fail to realize that their realm of expertise does not extend to the church. A staff member who lacks confidence is always changing his mind depending upon the ideas and values of the last church member with whom he has had a conversation. While confidence is extremely important, an even more valuable attribute is humility. A congregation desires a pastor and staff who do not perceive themselves above others.

Don Shula, the legendary former coach of the Miami Dolphins, tells a humorous story about himself. Coach Shula is a very humble man, but he remembers a day when he let his humility slip. He and his wife had retreated to a small town in Maine to avoid being noticed on their vacation. While there, they went to see a movie on a messy, rainy night. When Shula and his wife walked into the theater, the people began to applaud. The famous coach whispered to his wife, "I guess there's no place we can go where people won't recognize me." When they sat down, Shula shook hands with a man on their row and said, "I'm surprised that you know who I am." The man looked at him and replied, "Am I supposed to know who you are? We're just glad you came in because the manager said he wasn't going to start the movie unless there were at least ten people here." Just about the time we think we're something, somebody reminds us we're not![7]

Compassionate, Empathetic, Caring. Throughout the New Testament we learn that the demeanor of Christ is one of compassion. He has compassion for the multitude when they have no supper, and he responds by feeding the 5,000. He has compassion for the leper, reaching out his hand to the untouchable. Staff must emulate the compassion of Christ.

Friendly, Outgoing, Fun. While staff members do not have to appear as though they have just graduated from a Dale Carnegie seminar, they must be able to meet, greet, and interact with people. Ministers who take themselves too seriously do not seem genuine to the congregation. A genuine smile and a firm handshake are very effective tools for building relationships both at church and in the community. (I once heard church members complain that their pastor was friendly at church but ignored them in the grocery store.)

Appropriate. Acting appropriately is difficult to define. It entails all the measures necessary to make sure the pastor and staff respond in a logical and reasonable fashion. Telling jokes at the graveside of a dear saint is probably not appropriate. Asking the chairman of the deacon fellowship if you can borrow his jeep for a weekend excursion is most likely not appropriate. Some people instinctively seem to know what is appropriate, while others, seemingly, are clueless. Search for staff members who know how to be appropriate.

Admirable, Professional, Respectable, Confidential. Each staff member should be a professional in his field. He must know the importance of being confidential in regard to the conversations he has with church members. People are anxious to volunteer to help those whom they admire and respect.

Honest, Fair. Some time ago an article in *National Racquetball Magazine* told the story of Reuben Gonzales who was in the final match of a professional racquetball tournament. It was Gonzales' first shot at a victory on the pro circuit, and he was playing the perennial champion. In the fourth and final game, at match point, Gonzales made a super "kill" shot into the front wall to win it all. The referee called it good. One of the two linesmen affirmed that the shot was in. But Gonzales, after a moment's hesitation, turned around, shook his opponent's hand, and declared that his shot had "skipped" into the wall, hitting the court floor first. As a result, he lost the match. He walked off the court. Everyone was stunned. The next issue of *National Racquetball Magazine* displayed Reuben Gonzales on its front cover. The story searched for an explanation of this first-ever occurrence on the professional racquetball circuit. Who could ever imagine it in any sport or endeavor? A player, with everything officially in his favor, with victory in his hand, disqualified himself at match point and lost! When asked why he did it, Reuben said, "It was the only thing I could do to maintain my integrity."[8]

Once a staff member has been caught being dishonest, it is very difficult for the congregation to respect and trust that minister again. Likewise, if a group within the congregation perceives that a staff member is "playing favorites" with other church members, then his ministry will be derailed. Staff must strive to treat everyone fairly.

Peaceful, Authentic, Forgiving. While extroverted staff members are often effective, church members also desire genuine authenticity and peacefulness in their ministers. A sincere and forgiving leader models the love of Christ to church members in a tangible fashion.

Approachable. The congregation must feel comfortable communicating its concerns. When church members feel as though they will not be heard by a staff member, they cease to share their thoughts and feelings. Ministers who shun or ignore the members will never prove effective in ministry.

Conclusion

The congregation will respond to the leadership of an outstanding staff team. Investing energy and effort seeking the very best ministers is one of the wisest uses of a pastor's time. When employment decisions are made in haste, resources are wasted by trying to micromanage and eventually replace mediocre ministers. Every church staff member must be a model of commitment, integrity, and hard work. She must be loyal, timely, dependable, encouraging, visionary, flexible, humble, confident, friendly, honest, and confidential. Along with the pastor, the church staff will determine the future of the congregation.

Notes

[1]Charles H. Spurgeon once said, "You must be able to bear criticism, or you are not fit to be at the head of a congregation; and you must let the critic go without reckoning him among your deadly foes, or you will prove

yourself a mere weakling." See "The Blind Eye and the Deaf Ear," in *O Timothy* 11/7 (1994): 4.

[2]I learned this after I discovered that one candidate had listed his brother-in-law under the disguise of "former employer."

[3]Check with legal counsel before giving a negative reference.

[4]Check in advance with legal counsel in regard to the proper acquisition and utilization of credit information.

[5]"Improving Your Memory," *Speaker's Idea File* (September 1994): 4.

[6]Kevin Conrad, "The Holiest Word," *Sermon Notes and Illustrations* (November/December 1995): 7.

[7]"Attitudes," John Ortberg, Seeds Tape Ministry #M9733.

[8]Dennis Waitley, "Being the Best," *Bits and Pieces* (12 October 1995): 2.

Avoid using gimmicks.

The generational conflicts that center upon hymnals versus overhead screens, hymns versus choruses, and ties versus T-shirts are not the primary focus of this chapter. While I recognize that it is difficult—if not impossible—to separate the message from the method, I am concerned more with the content of worship than the elements of worship. The tendency of contemporary worship to be irreverent, human-centered, and void of apostolic theology is the concern—not the contemporary style itself. Traditional worship, moreover, is not necessarily God-centered or theologically grounded in the teaching of the early church.[1] In order to create a multi-generational worship experience, our services at First Baptist Church of Amarillo blend traditional and contemporary elements together in a complementary fashion.[2]

Church growth based upon solid theological principles is not the result of a circus.[3] The irony is thick: the church is trying to become like the world in order to attract the world. The attempt to be relevant to baby boomers has seduced some congregations into bringing "profane elements" of popular culture into sacred places. Lendol Calder of Augustana College relates the time when a Lutheran pastor invited his congregation to execute "the Wave" one Sunday morning.[4] The irony is that the world is not looking for a church like itself. The world is searching for the Kingdom of God—a Kingdom in which things are completely different from the kingdom of the present age. Beware of featuring dancing bears in order to draw a crowd. The old adage, "Whatever it takes to get 'em, you'll have to do more to keep 'em," is certainly true. Church growth based upon gimmicks is not likely to have lasting results.

Attract without compromising.

Examples of the dancing bear technique come across my desk at an alarming rate. For example, one brochure explained:

> Dr. and Mrs. Bob Smith present "Thank the Lord for Children Ministries," Christian outreach featuring heart-warming messages illustrated with live exotic animals. Federally licensed, insured, and available nationwide. Over 100,000 children brought to Christ and the local church. The program lasts one full hour and includes a rapidly paced presentation of over two dozen live animals in an up-close but safe setting that adults and children will never forget. At the close of each "Thank the Lord for Children" program, many children meet Jesus Christ, many for the first time.[5]

A camel, horse, leopard, lion, zebra, bear, cougar, and tiger are pictured on the promotional piece. As one of my pastor friends declared, "When we present Christianity as a circus, it's no wonder the world depicts us as charlatans selling snake oil from a covered wagon on the side of the road!"

How about this one? A Baptist church promoted an "Outdoor Extravaganza—Fun for the Entire Family." At this event you will:

> (1) See a master's trophy collection, which includes trophy mounts of the largest whitetails that have ever lived over the past 132 years. Most world records will be on display, including the "Hole in the Horn Buck." (2) View the most extraordinary display of domestic and exotic wildlife mounts ever assembled. You will have to see it to believe it. (3) Hold your breath as you watch the South Texas Snake Handlers and their amazing show. (4) View exhibits from area merchants and organizations geared to the great outdoor man or woman. (5) Bid in a silent auction full of lots

of great buys for everyone. How does a new boat sound? Perhaps a hunting or fishing trip of your dreams? (6) Attend seminars scheduled through the day—varmint calling, horn rattling. (7) See the Catfish Tank full of hungry fish for your youngster to reel in. (8) Climb a velcro wall for those who are brave enough to try the wall.[6]

This church seemed to promise everything short of allowing the participants to be baptized in a tank with the world's largest bass.

On 13 May 1991 *The Wall Street Journal* reported that in a Sunday service of one of America's largest evangelical churches, a wrestling match was held between church employees. "To train for the event, ten brave employees got lessons from Tugboat Taylor, a former professional wrestler, in pulling hair, kicking shins, and tossing bodies around without doing harm."[7] No harm to the staff members, perhaps, but what is the spiritual damage to the church itself from such a misplaced exhibition? I've also been informed by an eyewitness that this same congregation had a Fourth of July celebration that included a parade, fireworks exploding in the sanctuary, and Olympic gold medalist Mary Lou Retton turning somersaults across the platform.

Another *Wall Street Journal* article, dated 11 December 1990, profiled a large evangelical church in the Southwest that has taken the entertainment philosophy to the extreme. After sending staff members to study live, special effects at Bally's casino in Las Vegas, this church installed a half-million-dollar special effects system in its main auditorium. Now smoke, fire, sparks, and laser lights can be produced to accent the key points in the pastor's messages. The article described how the pastor concluded one service by ascending to "heaven" via invisible wires that drew him up, out of sight, while the choir and orchestra added the musical accompaniment to the smoke, fire, and light show. The Pentecostal Peter Pan act apparently was just a typical Sunday show for that pastor. According to the article, the pastor

> packs his church with such special effects as cranking up a chainsaw and toppling a tree to make a point . . .; the biggest Fourth of July fireworks display in town; and a Christmas service with a rented elephant, kangaroo, and zebra. The Christmas show features 100 clowns with gifts for the congregation's children.[8]

A more subtle example might hit closer to home. A church Christmas program in the Dallas/Fort Worth metroplex was featured in *U.S.A. Today* as the "Broadway of Christendom." This church pulls out all the stops, staging a show that is more production than pageant. The Christmas carnival includes clowns on stilts and an elephant that waves from the stage. Three wise men atop camels, five sheep, and a donkey appear later in the event. This production is on a scale twice the size of the average Broadway production. It's a three-hour holiday extravaganza for which tickets are sold for $10-13 each. Regarding the logic behind such hype, the church concluded, "Even people who never go to church will come, and the church has tried to make it an event they won't forget."[9]

The unchurched, no doubt, are not likely to forget a production costing $250,000 and incorporating 850 cast and crew members, flying angels soaring 40 feet above the stage, and wise men with vainglorious capes stretching more than 17 feet long (second only to Princess Diana's wedding dress train). But will this Christmas extravaganza communicate the gospel of a simple, first-century Jewish rabbi, a carpenter by trade, who had no place to lay his head and who refused the glamour and the glory of an earthly kingdom to die on a cross?

I am certainly aware of how tempting it is to employ side-show evangelism, to pull out the gimmicks that will give church attendance a sudden surge.[10] Promise Barney at

Vacation Bible School and watch your numbers double. Bring in the muscle team that features grown men busting bricks on their brawny chests, ripping phone books apart, and rebuking the devil and watch the teens flock to your church. I once attended a church service where an old man challenged two whip-driven horses to try to pull his arms apart. They could not—I witnessed. He then allowed a spectator to drive a Volkswagen Beetle across his chest. Seemingly, this modern-day Samson was unharmed by these capers, and he proclaimed that his strength was found in the Lord. Though I did not see him, I also once heard about a literally flaming evangelist. As he preached on the heat of hell, he would ignite himself, becoming a human torch before the eyes of a now-fearful congregation. All such gimmick evangelism is easy to employ and promises instant results.

The paradox of such pageantry is clear: Jesus never used gimmicks to draw a crowd. In fact, after performing his healing miracles, he often said to the beneficiary, "Be sure that you tell no one."[11] In the Gospel of John, moreover, following the feeding of the 5,000, the crowd was ready to make Jesus king because of his wonderful manna from heaven. Jesus, however, knew of their populist intentions and escaped. His sermon that followed was so challenging that, instead of recruiting disciples, Jesus actually drove them away. After so many followers were unwilling "to walk with him anymore," Jesus even challenged the Twelve: "You do not want to go away also, do you?" (John 6:67). Our Lord never compromised his method or his message in order to excite the multitudes. Jesus said to would-be disciples, "You'd better think long and hard before you choose to follow me because, if you follow in the footsteps of the Messiah, you'll find yourself on a cross."[12] He wants us to count the cost of discipleship because he demands our all. His challenge to the rich young ruler—"Sell all that you have and give it to the poor"—was because he knew this would be the most difficult test available for the young man.

Be God-friendly.

Dancing bears will draw a crowd, but is entertainment the goal of worship? We have become so focused on being "seeker-sensitive" that we have neglected believers. More importantly, we have forgotten God. Where the philosophy espousing worship as *entertainment* for *unbelievers* originated, I cannot be sure. I am sure, however, that it is neither biblical nor was it the practice of the early saints.

The biblical pattern is for the church to gather for worship and edification and then to scatter for evangelism. Our Lord's Great Commission begins with the word "*Go!*" As Ralph Wood points out, many churches today are missing the point of worship. We are not to engage in worship in order to get something from God. Rather, worship is to "give Him honor and praise for His unsurpassable worth."[13]

Our "user-friendly" tactics might not be "God-friendly." We have replaced theocentric praise of God with anthropocentric utilitarianism.[14] Brief sermonettes, multimedia presentations, and soul-soothing songs that focus on felt needs fail to be the worship of the gathered body of believers bowing before the mysterious throne of an almighty God. While efforts to "meet people right where they are" are important parts of many ministries within the church, they should never be the focus of worship.[15] As Marva J. Dawn concludes, "It is a misnomer to call services 'worship' if their purpose is to attract people rather than to adore God."[16]

David Wells argues that postmodern worship begins with our anxiety, pain, and disillusionment with the world in its disorder, with the family or marriage in its brokenness, or with the work place in its brutality and insecurity. God, therefore, is valued only to the extent that "He is able to bathe these wounds, assuage these insecurities, calm these fears, restore some sense of internal order, and bring some sense of wholeness."[17]

Worship should always be God-ward and not human-ward.[18] As Wood states, "Despite their much-touted success, most contemporary forms of worship are, I believe, premised on a deadly fallacy: the notion that the value of worship depends on our 'getting something out of it.' "[19] The entertainment nature of much of contemporary worship deceives us about who God is. We treat His nature, His name, and His Word with such frivolity that what was once a covenant community focused upon a crucified and resurrected Savior has become little more than a casual meeting permeated with "the sentiment that nothing extraordinary is going on, that what is happening is a gathering of ordinary people enjoying the experience of community."[20] The preeminent quality of much of contemporary worship is sentimentality that is, as C. S. Lewis put it, "an excess of emotion built on a false estimate of its object." True sentiment, on the other hand, "esteems things properly, loves them rightly, and orders them truly."[21] The sentimentality of much of our worship today encourages a perpetual adolescence of faith.

Gene Veith wrote in *Modern Reformation* that he had discovered the early church was in no way market-driven and was certainly not predisposed to make belief in Christ "user-friendly." Converts, rather, had to go through extensive, lengthy catechesis—an examination before they were accepted for baptism. In fact, the fear of persecution and even death served as the ultimate barrier to new member assimilation. Incredibly, though, by the power of the Holy Spirit, the church spread like wildfire. We are always tempted to preach what people want to hear. The homiletical principle guiding much of seeker-sensitive sermonizing is selection based on "user-friendliness." We pick and choose teachings from the Bible that correspond to our own culture's likes and interests.[22]

Unlike the call of antiquity to costly discipleship, modern worship often trivializes the sacred. William H. Willimon has best depicted this tendency in worship:

When culture is in the market for self-gratification and self-centeredness, we have been all too willing to give it what it thought it wanted. When asked, "Why worship?" we are quick to point out all the valuable benefits of worshiping God. While few enlightened Christians admit to the crudity of expecting God to give them a Mercedes in appreciation for an hour in church, they nevertheless do expect "inspiration" or, at a minimum, "a warm feeling" on Sunday morning.[23]

Willimon criticized the tendency of congregations to market themselves by peddling worship as fellowship, therapy, stress management, intellectual stimulation, or a pep rally. In each of these depictions of worship,

The focus is on me, my feelings, my commitments, my guilt, my needs. I am the center of worship, the focus of a carefully orchestrated series of Sunday morning activities that are designed to do something to or for me. We are so busy looking at ourselves, no wonder we sometimes miss God.[24]

The local church has an endless string of dancing bears who promise to meet "felt needs." We have forgotten about focusing on God.

Lenny Seidel correctly has argued that the gospel should not be presented in an entertainment mode. The Gospel is about a person—the Lord Jesus Christ—and nothing about his life was entertaining. Seidel has concluded that by and large church music written today has been corrupted by hedonism and subjectivism. The focus is now on the individual worshiper rather than on a Holy God. The result is a flood of music characterized by weak theology and designed to make people "feel good."[25] Much of church music today is driven by the bottom-line goals of Nashville CEOs who cannot be expected to be concerned about long-term results.[26] As John

Blanchard says in his book, *Pop Goes the Gospel,* "The life of Jesus was not a religious roadshow. He did not come to give a performance, but to give his life."[27]

David Wells, Professor of Theology at Gordon-Cornwell Theological Seminary, critically analyzed postmodern Christian music by examining the 406 praise songs contained in *Worship Songs of the Vineyard* and *Maranatha! Music Praise Chorus Book.* When compared to the hymns of classical spirituality, as represented in the 622 hymns of *The Covenant Hymnal,* the praise choruses of postmodern spirituality were theological weaklings. He concluded,

> The large majority of praise songs I analyzed, 58.9 percent, offer no doctrinal grounding or explanation for the praise; in the classical hymnody examined it was hard to find hymns that were not predicated upon and did not develop some aspect of doctrine.[28]

Not only were the praise choruses void of theological grounding, but they also privatized worship. While 21.6 percent of classical hymns were explicitly about the church, only 1.2 percent of the praise songs mentioned the collective people of God.[29] Wells has carefully quantified what many of us have known to be true—many praise choruses offer shallow, self-centered theology at best.[30] Remember, our concern must center on theological issues and not stylistic changes. I am *not* criticizing contemporary tunes or projectors; I am criticizing a genre of music focused on humanity rather than on God, on psychological wholeness rather than on sin and a Savior.[31]

Maurice Irvin raises the point that we may never get people to come to our churches unless we make our activities attractive and appealing to them, but he questions what we have accomplished if in doing so we get a building full of people who are not genuinely aware of the "awesome, glorious presence of God."[32] Modern-day church growth extravaganzas have brought shame to the bride of Christ. Like the money-changers in the Temple turned it into a den of thieves, we have turned the house of God into a three-ring circus rather than a place of reverence and worship. We have profaned the holy and "Broadway-ized" the sacred. Converts of the circus don't hang around very long after the tent has been taken down! If it takes a clown and cotton candy to bring them, it will take a two-headed camel to keep them.

Conclusion

Church growth that produces lasting results is not based upon glitter and glamour but upon formulating programs that meet real needs, upon teaching the apostles' theology, and upon the transforming power of prayer. The testimony of scripture reveals there was certainly a time when Jesus was tempted to use the "dancing bear" method. He was urged to draw a crowd with a spectacular splash. He was tempted to avoid the way of the cross and to go the way of miraculous mass marketing. Who was the tempter? Satan. What was the temptation? The temptation of the dancing bear.[33]

Satan took Jesus to the pinnacle of the Temple and urged him to jump. He said,

> If you are the Son of God, throw yourself down, for it is written, "He will give His angels charge concerning you, and on their hands they shall bear you up lest you strike your foot against a stone." (Matt 4:6)

Jumping from the pinnacle of the Temple, being rescued by angels, and enjoying the great acclamation of the crowd would certainly be preferable to a crown of thorns and nail-pierced feet. No matter how many lights we wrap around it, no matter how much glitter we try to glue over it, the central symbol of Christianity is the cross.[34] It is sacrifice; it is denial; it is being cursed and having to suffer.

Those things are hard to portray with the glamour of Broadway or the showtime of Branson. Are we having Miss America give her testimony because she truly is a humble individual who is beautiful in the likeness of Christ, or are we providing a circus sideshow? Is the famous quarterback's testimony done in sincerity and truth, or are we putting on a pageant? Be careful. Watch your motives. Gimmicks will always ultimately disappoint.

Frederica Mathewes-Green asserts that the biggest challenge to the church will come from within. She questions,

> Hearing the multitudes cry for safety, comfort and approval, will we be seduced into supplying only that? Will those renegades who persist in speaking of sin and repentance embarrass us till their unfashionable voices are silenced? Will the church of the new millennium put a happy face on the cross? It will sell like crazy; no doubt about it. What will it cost?[35]

We must emphasize theology over entertainment. We must retrace our steps to a worship focused on the Creator and not the created. An episode of the comic strip, *Peanuts*, illustrates the point: Lucy and Linus are looking out the window at hard rain. Lucy says, "What if it floods the whole earth?" Linus answers, "It will never do that. In the ninth chapter of Genesis God promised Noah that would never happen again." Lucy responds, "You've taken a great load off my mind." And Linus replies, "Sound theology has a way of doing that."

While few pastors are professional theologians, we all must proclaim the apostles' theology.[36] According to David Dunlap,

> The word of God regularly reminds readers of the crucial importance of both sound doctrine and solid teaching. The word doctrine is used forty-nine times in the New

Testament, and the closely related word teaching is used ninety-three times. The New Testament authors place clear emphasis upon these notions.[37]

On the occasion of his formal farewell to his students in Bonn, just before his expulsion from Germany in 1935, Karl Barth declared, "And now the end has come. So listen to my piece of advice: exegesis, exegesis, and yet more exegesis! Keep to the word, to the Scripture that has been given to us."[38] The church needs to repent. We have replaced the consuming fire with a mild-mannered God, the worship of the invisible God with forms of human invention, the moral law of God with the fulfillment of felt needs.[39] Smoke, laser light shows, and breaking bricks on brawny chests might be entertaining, but they have little to do with the theology of the New Testament. Dancing bears will draw a crowd, but be prepared: it will take more to keep them. We cannot compromise Jerusalem in order to marry Rome!

Notes

[1] Traditional worship is rarely criticized, however, for shallow theology. Rather, traditional worship is most often criticized for being irrelevant and unappealing.

[2] I have many concerns about worship designed to appeal to only one generation. This hyperdelineation of market segments does not allow for the multigenerational approach to doing church that the New Testament espouses. Paul instructs Timothy to treat older men as his father, younger men as his brothers, older women as his mother, and younger women as his sisters. This "family image" of church is hardly fulfilled in a community of faith that designs worship to appeal only to a single generation. Younger worshipers should seek to develop an appreciation for the traditions of their parents and grandparents (including hymns), while older worshipers should embrace the fresh ideas of younger generations (including drama). See also Paul Westermeyer, "Professional Concerns Forum: Chant, Bach, and Popular Culture," *The American Organist* 27/11 (November 1993):

35. Westermeyer argues that selecting church music to relate to one generation—usually baby boomers—flies in the face of the nature of the church, which should transcend all lines of age, race, gender, and economic status.

³Bobby Dagnel, pastor of First Baptist Church, Nederland, Texas, contributed substantially to the contents of this chapter.

⁴Lendol Calder, "Religion and Pop Culture: The Limitation of Liturgical Karaoke," *Family Policy* (July/August 1998): 13. See also Lendol Calder, "Christian Karaoke: Why Are Some Evangelicals Going 'High Church'?" *Touchstone* (March/April 1998): 11-12. Calder concluded that contemporary-style churches have rejected "tradition" but have refused to nurture a robust culture of their own, a culture rooted in the Scriptures. The unintended result has been, and continues to be, the uncritical adoption of the dominant culture of their host society, which in the case of Americans would be the culture of consumption. For a more positive treatment of contemporary worship, see Charles Trueheart, "Welcome to the Next Church," *Atlantic Monthly* 278/2 (August 1996): 37-58.

⁵Actual wording from brochure. Names changed.

⁶For obvious reasons, the church's name is not given. This promotional language was taken from the church's own brochure.

⁷R. Gustav Niebuhr, "Megachurches Strive To Be All Things to All Parishioners," *The Wall Street Journal*, 13 May 1991, A1, 5.

⁸Robert Johnson, "Preaching a Gospel of Acquisitiveness, A Showy Sect Prospers," *The Wall Street Journal*, 11 December 1990, A1.

⁹Deborah Sharp, "In Dallas, a Pageant That Soars," *USA Today*, 17 December 1997, 3A.

¹⁰I will be the first to admit that there is often a fine line between a successful program and a "dancing bear." We have to struggle with this distinction on a daily basis at First Baptist Church.

¹¹For examples of the "messianic secret," see Matt 8:4 and Mark 1:44; 5:43; 7:36.

¹²Implied from the text of Mark 8:34-37; Matt 10:28, 39; 16:24-26; 20:23; and John 20:17-19.

¹³For a discussion concerning the move from adoration of God to entertainment of men in Roman Catholic worship, see Richard John Neuhaus, "At Ease in Zion," *First Things* 85 (August/September 1998): 80-82.

¹⁴Leander Keck, *The Church Confident* (Nashville: Abingdon Press, 1993) 34.

¹⁵Ralph Wood, "The Fallacy of Getting Something Out of Worship," *The Christian Ministry* 28/2 (March/April 1997): 16-17. For the watershed article in Pauline studies that argues against a psychologizing of the apostle's theology, see Krister Stendahl, "The Apostle Paul and the Introspective Conscience of the West," *Harvard Theological Review* 56/3 (1956): 204.

For an excellent review of the issues that surface in comprehending Paul's theology, see Robert B. Sloan, "Paul and the Law: Why the Law Cannot Save," *Novum Testamentum* 33/1 (1991): 35-60.

[16]Marva J. Dawn, *Reaching Out Without Dumbing Down* (Grand Rapids: Eerdmans, 1995) 81.

[17]David F. Wells, *Losing Our Virtue: Why the Church Must Recover Its Moral Vision* (Grand Rapids: Eerdmans, 1998) 42.

[18]Not all contemporary worship leaders are unaware of the need for worship to be God-centered. For example, see Louie Giglio, *Into His Presence* (Choice Worship Resources, 1996).

[19]Wood, 16.

[20]Wood, 18, quoting Peter Berger.

[21]Wood, 18.

[22]Gene Veith, "Cambridge Highlights," *Modern Reformation* (July/August 1996): 6.

[23]William H. Willimon, *The Bible: A Sustaining Presence in Worship* (Valley Forge PA: Judson Press, 1981) 30-31.

[24]Ibid.

[25]Calder, 14. Paul L. Lusher, a church musician who directs the Center for Church Music in Grand Haven, Michigan, believes the sheer ease of appropriating forms of popular culture in worship helps explain their success. The more traditional approach to worship and music requires far more preparation and training on the part of both leaders and participants: "Just as a fast food outlet can deliver a meal at less cost and effort than a five-star restaurant, a contemporary church can order a freshly-minted service without near the kind of aesthetic awareness and musical expertise that a more traditional public worship demands."

[26]Lenny Seidel, "Music in Worship: Demanding a Distinction," *Voice Magazine* 74/5 (September/October 1995): 10-11. See also Tim Ellsworth, "Singer Calls for Christian Music Reformation," *The Baptist Standard* 110/1 (7 January 1998): 1, 3. In this article Christian recording artist Steve Camp issues a call for reformation in the contemporary Christian music industry. Camp has observed that in the past several years there has been a not-so-subtle drifting away from Christ-centered music to human-centered music. Camp argues that Christian music has become more of a business and less of a ministry. Camp describes contemporary Christian music as "for the moment, but not for eternity." He continues, "Transitory, temporal, trivial messages that devalue deity and raise 'felt-need' affairs above eternal 'real-need' concerns produced disposable, consumer-driven, cotton-candy music."

[27]John Blanchard, *Pop Goes the Gospel* (Hertfordshire, England: Evangelical Press, 1983) 114.

[28]Wells, 44. Leander Keck, in *The Church Confident*, 88, said the "ditties" that we now sing in worship make "a nursery rhyme sound like Thomas Acquinas."

[29]Compare James Hunter, *Evangelism: The Coming Generation* (Chicago: University of Chicago Press, 1987) 65. Hunter analyzed releases from eight of the most prolific evangelical publishers and found that 97.8 percent of their titles concerned the self in "an accentuation of subjectivity and the virtual veneration of the self, exhibited in deliberate efforts to achieve self-understanding, self-improvement, and self-fulfillment."

[30]Marva J. Dawn, in *Dumbing Down*, 87, concludes, "A principal cause of such dumbing down is the contemporary confusion of praise with 'happiness.' Some worship planners and participants think that to praise God is simply to sing upbeat music; consequently, many songs that are called 'praise' actually describe the feelings of the believer rather than the character of God. In the extreme, a focus on good feelings distorts the truth of the gospel into a 'health, wealth, and victory' therapy. We must recognize this for the idolatry it is. Centering on happiness makes us forget that the world gains redemption not through the church's glory but through Christ's sacrifice and the suffering of God's people."

[31]At times Wells seems to cross the line and criticize the method rather than the message of contemporary worship. See *Losing Our Virtue*, 206. He, for example, assumes that drama is always amusing when, in fact, properly done, drama can be a strong vehicle of prophetic rebuke.

[32]Maurice R. Irvin, "Man-Centered or God-Centered?" *Alliance Life* 131/8 (10 April 1996): 28. Also, Mark Noll argues that we cannot claim victory simply because evangelical churches are full while mainline churches are experiencing decline. He appeals for Christian scholarship and critical thinking. See Mark Noll, *The Scandal of the Evangelical Mind* (Grand Rapids: Eerdmans, 1994) 29.

[33]According to Richard B. Hays, "Clinging to the Word," *The Christian Century* 109/5 (5-12 February 1992): 124, "Satan, trying to recruit Jesus, offers an attractive package: bread, power, fame. The lure is real. Jesus is hungry in the wilderness, wrestling with a vocation sure to lead to suffering and death. The devil offers a way out, offers perks, proposes the big splash in the big media market. After the temple-pinnacle skywalking trick, the endorsement offers will roll in. ('Is it the shoes?') Who could resist?"

[34]Ralph Wood, in "The Fallacy," 17, argued, "Because it should express the glory of God, worship should minister to people where they ought to be. There we seek not to have our needs satisfied but to have them redefined in light of the cross and the resurrection."

35Frederica Mathewes-Green, "Happy Hour," *Current Thoughts and Trends* 12/9 (September 1996): 2.

³⁶The apostles' theology as evidenced from the sermons in Acts and other New Testament hymns and creeds can be summarized as the following: (1) that God had powerfully acted for our salvation through the life, and especially the death and resurrection, of one Jesus of Nazareth; (2) that this same Jesus was now enthroned at the right hand of God, having been exalted following his resurrection to the status of supreme heavenly Lord, now sharing the titles and prerogatives of Yahweh Himself; (3) that this same Jesus had poured forth his Spirit upon all his followers; (4) that all who would come to him in a humility of trust and obedience, declaring him Lord and following him in an initiatory ceremony of baptism, would not only be his people, but also find the salvation long anticipated by the Jewish prophets; (5) that such salvation would constitute the followers of Jesus as the authentic and regathered Israel of God; (6) that this same Jesus would come again, manifesting himself in heavenly glory to all the earth, thereby bringing to a final conclusion this present evil age and ushering in the long-awaited age to come; and (7) that all of these dramatic saving events were accomplished in fulfillment of the ancient (Jewish) Scripture. Robert Sloan, "Preaching and the New Testament," in *Handbook of Contemporary Preaching*, edited by Michael Duduit (Nashville: Broadman Press, 1992) 321

³⁷David Dunlap, "In Defense of Doctrine," *Uplook* 64/4 (April 1997): 18-20.

³⁸Eberhard Busch, *Karl Barth: His Life from Letters and Autobiographical Texts* (Philadelphia: Fortress Press, 1976) 259.

³⁹Robert Godfrey, "Cambridge Highlights," *Modern Reformation* (July/August 1996): 6.

Develop programs that meet needs.

For the past five years the Buttercup program at Stanley Avenue United Methodist Church has had a very difficult time electing officers.[1] Its primary purpose in the church is to prepare young ladies (ages 13-18) for involvement in the Women's Circle. Attendance has steadily declined since 1980. Only the pastor's daughters and the Smith and Langley girls—who attend church every time the doors are open—were present for the last meeting.

The church's dynamic youth program, under the leadership of the new youth minister, Terri Stanton, has steered the girls' interests into exciting, new ministries such as "Prime Time Live," an hour of fun, games, and multimedia communication, and "WorldTeam," a missions-centered program that involves conducting summer backyard Bible studies in underprivileged neighborhoods. The decline in the Buttercups' attendance is in no way an indication that the young ladies are no longer interested in church, Bible study, or missions activities. Rather, they are just not interested in dressing up, sipping hot tea, and eating sugar cookies as they plan ministry activities. It has become increasingly difficult to recruit young ladies to attend this outdated, formal approach to ministry when more contemporary and exciting alternatives are available.

Mrs. Brunchfield has done her best to reenergize the Buttercups. She faithfully calls all the young ladies on the roster and makes speeches at each monthly Buttercup meeting, holding high the tradition and heritage of 100 years of Buttercup badges. She has even attempted to shame the mothers of the teenage girls into making their daughters attend. Despite her efforts, the bottom line has remained the same: the girls simply are no longer interested in the Buttercup ministry.

In reality, the Buttercup organization is dead, but everyone has refused to bury it. While this was a very successful ministry during the 1950s and 1960s, the decline has been slow but steady. All of the time and energy currently expended on the Buttercups is simply prolonging the intensive-care period for a dying program. Mrs. Brunchfield is committed to saving the Buttercups when there is no reason to continue the program's existence. The youth have found alternatives for doing both Bible study and ministry activities. Insisting that the girls attend the Buttercup banquet is the equivalent of insisting that a teenager ride in a one-horse surrey while a red sports sedan awaits.

Churches become easily attached to a program, to the status quo, and they fail to continually evaluate their program offerings based upon whether those programs are actually meeting someone's needs. Denominational leaders, especially in mainline denominations, are guilty of sending a flood of programs down the denominational pipeline, expecting their congregations to open a local franchise for those programs without considering whether they will actually meet the needs of that particular community of faith.

Survey needs.

If a program has been adequately planned in terms of leadership, literature, location, and scheduling and yet does not attract church members, then you can be sure people do not feel as though this program will meet any of their needs. A church that insists on continually offering the same dated programs, despite the fact that the congregation obviously has no interest in them, is like a merchant who insists on peddling the same old products, despite the fact that people are no longer willing to purchase them. While the ice man stopped peddling his frozen wares decades ago, churches still promote programs that are not meeting contemporary needs. Both the stagnant church and the stagnant merchant will soon find themselves "out of business."

We should never change programs that are working effectively, but too often there is a great reluctance to discard dated programs that, in reality, are meaningless to the current members of the congregation. A silent majority in the congregation find themselves walking through the same old mazes for the sake of a few members who don't want to make changes because "the way things have always been is the way things should stay!"

Churches should continually evaluate all of their programs based on whether they are meeting the spiritual needs of the congregation. When programs fail to thrive, they must be gently pushed aside for new programs that will bring vitality into the community of faith. Whether or not a program is meeting needs can be determined by the interest of the congregation. If members must be pushed and prodded to participate and seem to do so out of a sense of obligation rather than a sense of excitement, then the program is more than likely failing to meet spiritual needs.

A program does not, however, need to attract great crowds in order to be considered effective. In fact, some programs patterned for small groups of people are actually doing a tremendous job in meeting needs. Effectiveness can be measured by the small group's intensity and enthusiasm for the program. For example, if your church's support group for those caring for aging parents is faithfully attended by a dozen members, then that program can be deemed a success because it has helped those individuals who have a real need. On the other hand, if a visitation program that was designed to help the entire congregation reach out to the community only attracts a handful of persons each week, then the program is not meeting the needs of enough members to be considered worthy of continuation. Churches must not continue a program only for the program's sake. Programs are for meeting the needs of people.

A soldier stood at attention in an isolated corner of the Russian palace. When questioned about his purpose, the soldier could only say he was following his captain's orders. The captain was summoned, and he too did not know the purpose for this guard but knew that regulations required it. Upon investigation it was discovered that a century earlier, Catherine the Great (empress from 1762 to 1796) had established the post to protect a newly planted rose bush. One hundred years later, guards were still being posted to keep watch over a barren spot of turf.[2] The point is clear: most things are worthy of doing for only a limited period of time—not forever.

Generate enthusiasm.

One of the oldest strategies for church growth is starting new Bible study units. Undoubtedly, these units attract more members than established classes. New groups have not yet formed a social substructure, and visitors feel completely welcomed and part of a new beginning. They are not threatened by existing relationships, habits, or patterns that stifle growth in established Bible study departments.

Church members and visitors currently seek more variety from church programming. Therefore, the old structure of one class per age group no longer satisfies the various needs people experience. This drive for more options is an outgrowth of the numerous choices consumers have in every realm of life. For example, we no longer simply consume Coke. Rather, we have Classic Coke, Caffeine-Free Classic Coke, Diet Coke, Diet Caffeine-Free Coke, and, for a while, we were even offered a New Coke. Wendy's is no longer just a hamburger establishment. Now, fast food connoisseurs can find hamburgers, chicken sandwiches, pitas, salads, chili, baked potatoes, spaghetti, Mexican chips and dip, and an extensive salad bar there. Perhaps tomorrow Wendy's will be offering pizza or shrimp![3]

This "menu mentality" has slowly made its way into the local congregation. In response the church can foster growth by offering alternatives during the traditional Bible study hour: a biblically-based divorce recovery class, a class focused on dealing with difficult people, a multi-age, in-depth Bible book study, or a marriage enrichment Sunday School class. This multilayered approach builds on the typical age-graded Bible study hour and attracts some individuals who would never consider attending a traditional Sunday School class.

When a visitor at First Baptist Church of Amarillo inquires as to which Sunday School class he should attend, I frequently respond with, "Well, you have several choices. I would encourage you to visit three or four classes before you select the one you feel will best meet your needs." Today a young couple visiting First Baptist Church can choose from the following: a traditional age-graded Sunday School class composed of young couples facing similar life struggles, an all-ages class with about 100 attenders taught by a local physician with a flair for emotional restoration and practical application, a "pastor's class" taught by our associate pastor that majors on exegetical expertise, a marriage enrichment class geared toward strengthening husband/wife relationships, or a class designed to help them deal with the difficult people in their lives. This "something for everyone" approach allows the traditional church to have more doors through which people may enter the Bible study hour.

Enlist member input and initiative.

The old denominational approach of assuming that everyone, despite different demographic backgrounds, will enjoy the same church programs is inadequate. A "franchise system" that sends a programming idea from a detached denominational official four states away to the local church is no longer acceptable. In fact, even the pastor and staff of the local church often are not the best sources of programming ideas. Rather, if the pastor and staff carefully listen to and evaluate the ideas and suggestions of the membership, there is a real possibility for success.

The most successful Bible study classes I have ever inaugurated resulted from individuals who explained they needed a new setting, a new teacher, and a new situation to meet their needs. The "pastor-down" approach risks the possibility of being totally irrelevant to the needs of the congregation. If the pastor thinks all left-handed people should attend a left-handed Sunday School department, he will have little success in establishing such a department. If, however, he discovers that several members desire a divorce recovery-centered Bible study, he can establish a successful new ministry. Often, persons will already have recruited a possible teacher when they approach the pastor and staff about beginning a new class. Let the congregation make your job easier!

Permitting members to shape the church's program menu gives programs a fair chance of finding an audience. Our Sunday evening program involves CARE groups (Caring About Real Experiences). Among a great variety of course selections—"Master Your Money," "Making Peace with Your Past," "Welcome to First Baptist Church," "Experiencing God," "Crisis Care: Hope for the Hurting," "Who Are These Crazy People Called Baptists?", "Learning To Share Your Faith," and "Raising Kids Who Turn Out Right"—the two most popular choices are money management and Baptist history. While I predicted that "Making Peace with Your Past" would attract more people than a study in denominational history, many of our people found a study of their denominational heritage to be interesting and informative.

Meet real needs.

No two churches are exactly alike, and programs that excel in one congregation may fail in another. Nonetheless, the following are programming examples for various segments of your congregation:[4]

Preschoolers. One preschool program that has met with great success at First Baptist is the "New Kid on the Pew." When a child turns five, she begins to attend the worship service with her parents. The week before the child's fifth birthday, the preschool minister sends a special card explaining that the child will receive a "New Kid on the Pew" bag and will have her picture taken on the following Sunday. In the bag the restless preschooler finds a "New Kid on the Pew" button, a small box of crayons, Kleenex, a pencil, and a Pastor's Pals booklet. The child is encouraged to draw pictures about the sermon each Sunday. The photograph of the child coming into church with her new bag in hand is published in the weekly church newsletter. This program is successful because it addresses a difficult, transitional time for both the preschooler and the parents. Preschool parents are reluctant to bridge that gap from nursery care to having their child present in a one-hour worship service. The "New Kid on the Pew" program recognizes this tension, makes provisions for an easier transition, and transforms what might otherwise be a dreaded time into a time to feel special.

Another overwhelmingly successful preschool and children's program is "Parent's Night Out." The church provides child care one Friday night each month so that parents can enjoy an evening to themselves. The cost is minimal; the care is excellent; and the children look forward to it as much as the parents do. Making this program available to non-members allows prospects to become familiar with your church's excellent preschool care. The preschool minister meets new families face to face and has an opportunity to invite them to other preschool events. Since many young couples live miles away from family, this has proven to be a program that meets a real need.

Children. Summer becomes a special time at our church with "Summer Daze." These are play days designed to keep children from developing a sense of boredom during the summer months. Children who have completed the first through the sixth grades are offered a variety of interesting field trips to local sites including a miniature golf course, a science center, a history museum, a roller skating rink, and an amusement park.

"Bible Drill" is an old program that is still meeting a need for many families. While very little of the contemporary educational process involves rote memory, "Bible Drill" challenges the student to be self-disciplined, to function under pressure, to memorize great quantities of material, and to become familiar with the Old and New Testaments. This program has a heightened sense of competition and allows students to progress from church Bible drills to statewide competitions within some denominations. While the program has been around for years, new approaches keep it fresh. The memory verses may be set to music using popular tunes with which the children are familiar. Committed participants emerge able to locate Bible books and to recite Scripture. How long does it take you to find the book of Obadiah? Bible drillers can locate it in ten seconds!

Youth. "D-Groups" are small mentoring groups that place an adult with six to eight teenagers, usually divided by age and gender. The purpose of this program is to promote spiritual growth through intimate relationships that support, challenge, and require accountability. Unlike curriculum-based Sunday School classes, these groups are relationship-centered. They meet on Sunday evenings for forty-five minutes to an hour. The members of a group hold each other accountable in areas such as quiet time, Scripture memorization, and moral behavior. Each and every D-Group meeting is unique since it tries to address challenges the teens have faced that particular week. The key to a successful D-Group is a devoted mentor who serves as a role model and builds a personal relationship with each teen in his or her group.

"Student Mission Initiative" (SMI) is a new program in our youth division. Upon returning from their spring break mission trip to Mexico each year, the youth ask the same question: "Why can't we do this type of ministry at home?" The goal of SMI is to involve our students weekly in ministry so they may realize that church is more about giving than receiving. Since this ministry is only available to students who will pledge a seventy-five percent attendance record, the teens also learn about responsibility and accountability. Students are required to attend a weekly meeting on Sunday evenings in which the "game plan" for the following Tuesday's Backyard Bible Club is developed. The Backyard Bible Club, which is held in an underprivileged area, includes stories from Scripture, crafts, and recreational games. To add a new dimension to the ministry, the SMI program is concluded with a "Stepping Out" day in which the entire youth group (even those not involved in SMI) goes into the neighborhood to serve by mowing lawns, cleaning windows, and helping out with small chores.

Another successful program is "Ministry to Students Away." One of the most difficult transitions in life is the great leap from the home to the university. The church should help make this transition as comfortable as possible. This is accomplished when church members travel to the campuses most attended by teens from their congregation. Taking students out to eat and listening to their concerns encourages them. Special interest can also be shown to the students during exam week by sending them care packages full of cookies, treats, and a personal note about the church's care and concern. Every college student dreams about getting mail in the often-too-empty post office box. This ministry shows concern for the students, and their families appreciate the church's extra effort.

Adults. A "Celebrating Your Marriage Weekend" provides young adults with an opportunity to spend several days with other couples in a learning/sharing event. Usually a guest is invited to lead the sessions. Sessions are both instructive and interactive—no lecture-only format. The weekend may be held in a hotel or retreat facility to allow for a minimum of distractions. The church could provide a list of child-care volunteers for couples who need assistance. Full or partial scholarships should also be made available for those who need them.

The "Young Businessmen's Lunch" is a program that allows men to meet, network, and fellowship together. It provides a great atmosphere for a Christian businessman to bring a friend to a nonthreatening or entry-level activity. The lunch group could meet weekly or monthly and could be led by a pastor, staff member, or layman. Devotional thoughts should be *very* relevant.

Single Adults. "Project 19:19" is a service program, based on Matthew 19:19, designed to foster singles serving singles. For example, our younger singles painted the house of an elderly single woman in our congregation. During December, Project 19:19 involves our singles caroling on the doorstep of our "in-home" singles and delivering them a Christmas gift. This is a quarterly program that will eventually include a yearly mission trip.

"Dinner for Eight," another successful singles program, allows single adults to meet married adults in the congregation. The monthly dinner groups consist of four single adults and two married couples. Singles desire meaningful relationships with the whole congregation, not just with other singles.

Senior Adults. The "In-Home Visitation" program serves elderly members well. Members who are no longer able to attend a church service may have many needs met by a personal visit from a member of the congregation. Senior adults who are confined to their homes often feel neglected; while they once enjoyed years of faithful service within their community of faith, no one seems to miss them any longer. Larger churches may use a computer database and a mapping program to assign in-home visitation team members monthly visits with three or four senior adults who live within the same geographical area.

Brad Creed, Dean of Truett Seminary, once defined a pastor as a person "who labors under the misconception that he can adequately care for the needs of more than 100 people." A "Hospital Follow-Up" ministry, conducted by and largely for senior adults, helps a pastor meet real needs within the congregation. While many patients receive too many visitors while in the hospital, they are often forgotten once their hospital stay is complete. By use of a computer database, a member's stay in the hospital can be tracked from admission to release. Each person who has been released from the hospital could receive a call from the follow-up team after two weeks, four weeks, six weeks, eight weeks, and then as necessary. The "Hospital Follow-up" ministry demonstrates that the church remembers and continues to care for its members.

Recreation. Continuing education opportunities have been very successful at First Baptist Church. Every church is filled with individuals who have a variety of talents and gifts. Our church tries to pair these teachers/leaders with potential students who have similar interests. We have offered everything from Internet surfing to fly fishing. The typical class meets once a week for four to eight weeks. One of our most popular classes was taught by a local interior designer who was willing to "share her secrets" with the men and women of the church who wanted tips on how to decorate their homes. Classes could also cover interests such as estate planning, self-defense, or Cajun style cooking.

With so many family restaurants catering to children's birthday parties, we've created our own "Birthday Party Adventure" utilizing our Family Life Center. With a variety of activities available—roller skating, basketball, volleyball, ping-pong, obstacle course, soft-play system, and a carnival moon bouncer—we allow the child to create his own unique party. We have designed an indoor soft-play system with colorful tubes and spiral slides that rivals even Discovery Zone. This recreational attraction is so large that parents can participate with their children. We even have a clown in full make-up to supervise the party adventure. The birthday child receives a specially designed T-shirt signed by all of his birthday guests, thus leaving the child with a collectible from his birthday adventure. The cost for the "Birthday Party Adventure" is just two dollars per child. This fee pays for the additional workers needed to supervise the party. Six to eight weeks before the birthday of a church member (sixth grade and under), we mail a card that encourages the child to book his "Birthday Party Adventure."

Seasonal specialties are a hit. During the "Sweet Sixteen" we have "The Road to the Final Few," our version of a three-on-three, "Hoop It Up" basketball tournament, scheduled the same Saturday as the NCAA "Final Four." With the offering of several different age and skill levels, this can be a successful family event. We created names for our divisions, for example, the Goliath Division for the most competitive and the Jehosha(fat) Division for the couch-potato types. The small entry fee guarantees each participant several games, a commemorative T-shirt, a sack lunch, and a whole lot of fun and fellowship. Other seasonal specialties might include a tennis tournament during the week of Wimbledon.

Music. The "All-Church Dinner Theatre" is a ticketed affair that provides both knee-slapping entertainment and a delicious meal. It involves the church staff and the music ministry. Held each evening from a Thursday through a Sunday, this is an excellent opportunity for members to invite prospects to a light-hearted and fun event that will appeal to all.

"Summer Music Camp" provides children with an opportunity to experience music within a more concentrated time frame. In addition to learning activities and music education, children are made more aware of the aspects of worship and the gospel. The camp, scheduled Monday through Friday mornings, is for first through sixth graders. Classes include choir, handbells, keyboard activities, arts and crafts, sign language, and lessons in music theory and appreciation. This day camp seeks to answer questions about worship, music, and special services such as the Lord's Supper and baptism. Sunday services following the music camp might be geared more specifically to children. A special children's bulletin could be prepared, and children could participate in music, prayers, and Scripture reading.

These are just a few examples that demonstrate what can be done when a church is willing to explore new programs and revitalize old ones to meet real needs. A church that continues to offer programs that do not meet the needs of members or prospects will soon find itself shrinking. People want to attend church where the pastor and staff offer programs that meet the real challenges of life. What is preached on Sunday morning ought to be relevant to our lives on Monday morning.

Conclusion

Churches must not become so attached to the status quo that they fail to evaluate their programs based upon whether those programs are actually meeting someone's spiritual needs. While church leaders should never change programs that are working effectively, they must listen to the programming ideas and suggestions of the membership. Permitting members to shape the church's program menu gives programs a fair chance of finding an audience. There is no reason to invest time and energy into a program that does not make a difference in the lives of the membership.

Notes

¹Fictitious example.

²*Ministry Management* 2/1: 1, as quoted in Raymond McHenry, "Purpose," *In Other Words* (Winter 1997): 15.

³Leonard Sweet, Dean of the Theological School at Drew University, reported that our "choice-driven" society now has nearly 20 different kinds of Kleenex, 40 different varieties of Tylenol, and more than 700 different makes and models of cars in the U.S. alone! See *A Cup of Coffee at the Soul Café* (Nashville: Broadman and Holman, 1998) 18.

⁴I would like to thank Elaine Clark, Linda Dudley, Don Vanderslice, Robby Barrett, Brian Seay, Lynn Garrett, Jordan Cox, Lanny Allen, and David Lowe for their help with programming suggestions. They are members of the staff ministry team at First Baptist Church of Amarillo and are keenly aware of the programming possibilities within their areas of expertise.

Devise an effective outreach program.

The same "faithful few" were showing up for outreach every Tuesday evening. We had a meal together, sorted through the yellowed prospect records that had not been updated in several years, and departed with somber, defeated spirits—a weekly outreach episode at First Baptist Church of Amarillo in 1996.

In sharp contrast, outreach is second only to Bible study in programming priority at First Baptist Church in 1998. As noted earlier, more than 400 people are enrolled in outreach on a monthly basis. Each week, about 90 people stream into our fellowship hall for a positive outreach experience. The records are accurate, up-to-date, user-friendly, and properly organized. The church staff members, absent from outreach in the past, are carefully stationed to assist church members with their assignments. The pastor sits at the front sign-in table, greeting and encouraging each participant.

During a decade in which many churches are silently phasing out their weekly outreach programs as a result of poor attendance and lackluster results, First Baptist Church of Amarillo is realizing unprecedented participation and proven results. A drastic rebirth has taken place in our outreach program. As a result, we have exchanged steady decline for steady growth. After having utilized the new outreach program for just one year, First Baptist Church received the "Fastest Growing Sunday School" award in the Amarillo Baptist Association and fourth largest attendance increase in the large church category of the Baptist General Convention of Texas. Energy properly invested into successful outreach programs produces real results.

Address past failure.

Why the transformation? We began by pondering: "Why are our members not willing to participate in outreach?" Deacons, Sunday School teachers, and otherwise active church members were noticeably absent from our outreach program. Why?

Unrealistic Expectations. Most churches make unrealistic time demands on their members. Traditional programs require church families to participate in Sunday morning Bible study and worship, Sunday evening worship, Tuesday visitation, and a Wednesday service of prayer and praise. Our members had already committed two nights each week to church activities even without outreach or committee responsibilities. The remaining evenings were filled with Little League, homework, and a host of other competing activities. The primary reason our members were not returning for outreach on Tuesday evening was clear: we were already demanding too much of their time for all of the other church programs, and their schedules were already overburdened.

Lack of Organization and Preparation. We also discovered that faithful church members were not participating in outreach because our prospect records were dated, unorganized, and difficult to understand. I remember one Tuesday evening when a physician glanced at a prospect card and then chuckled, "You call these newcomers? This family has lived in Amarillo for two years!"

Pastor's Failure To Prioritize. The third apparent reason was that until the pastor and staff made outreach a priority in their own schedules and in the church's spotlight, members were not going to perceive outreach as an important activity. People watch the pastor closely and follow his lead. I'll do almost anything to avoid missing outreach on Tuesdays, and I expect the same dedication from our staff.

Organize for success.

In our efforts to find an outreach program that addressed these three ingredients for failure, we made a visit to the West Jackson Baptist Church in Jackson, Tennessee.[1] We observed, discussed, took notes, and, in the end, modified that church's outreach program to meet the needs of our people. The basic tenets of the program are summarized as follows.

Realistic Expectations. Church members are divided into four teams. Each team is expected to be present only once each month. Thus, church members are asked to commit only twelve hours each year to outreach. While members receive a first, second, third, or fourth Tuesday of the month assignment, attendance is flexible; church members may actually attend any twelve Tuesday evenings each year. Team captains manage about twelve to fifteen church members and call them on the Monday preceding their assigned Tuesday evening of outreach. About one hundred people receive phone calls each week reminding them of their commitment to outreach. They are also reminded that if they are not available on their assigned Tuesday evening, they can make it up some other Tuesday during the month.

Manageable Assignments. We really do allow our people to accomplish their task within one hour's time. Two-person visitation teams are assigned no more than two names, usually within the same zip code. Letter writers are asked to write only four or five letters each week. We have kept our covenant with our people by telling them we truly only need twelve hours of their time each year in order to do outreach in an effective way.

Pastor's Priority. The pastor and staff lead the way. Unlike other participants, the pastor and staff are there each and every week, meeting with every team, helping in any way possible. Church members who observe their pastor and staff being committed to outreach are much more enthusiastic about engaging in outreach themselves. What we do in regard to outreach communicates more clearly than what we say. Our staff is present, enthusiastic, and busy doing various tasks to assist our team members with their outreach assignments.

Variety. A variety of tasks is available. When team members arrive, they are given the opportunity to visit either newcomers, absentees, or recent worship visitors. If they are not comfortable making visits, then they may make telephone calls to absentees, write letters to newcomers to our city, or even volunteer to provide child care for others who are participating in various outreach activities. Whatever activity our members choose, they are made to feel equally appreciated. Writing letters is just as important as visiting. Making child care available allows others to make contacts and is, thus, a vital part of outreach.

Nonconfrontational Approach. A nonconfrontational approach to evangelism is the key. Our people are not asked to evangelize according to any "cookie cutter" presentation. Rather, they are asked to deliver information about our church, show genuine care and concern, and be ready to answer questions in regard to their faith. The Holy Spirit, amazingly, provides the right team members on the right doorstep at the right time. A visit might entail simply dropping off a packet of information at the doorstep, or it may involve an in-depth discussion about how to become a disciple of Christ. The majority of our visits are intended to be brief, doorstep visits in which neither the visitor nor the prospect is put in an awkward position by an unscheduled "drop-in."

Accurate and Updated Files. Nothing frustrates outreach participants more than receiving dated or inaccurate information. Prospect files must come from accurate sources and be updated on a regular basis. Each assignment an outreach team receives should come with a record of all previous contacts and a map leading to the prospect's home with the correct location highlighted. This way, there is no guesswork. The outreach team is well prepared in every way possible to ensure a successful visit. After making a visit, it is crucial that those participating in outreach report their results so files can be updated for the next outreach team. Our church has employed a part-time secretary just to manage these prospect files.

Quality Promotional Materials. Our visitation teams are given an impressive package to deliver to each prospect. The promotional material is professionally produced, multi-colored, and attractively packaged in a First Baptist Church doorknob hanging bag. In the packet the prospect receives a free Wednesday evening meal ticket, a three-month membership (or twenty-four visits) to our Family Life Center, and information on just about every facet of life at First Baptist Church. In fact, we have recently added a professional quality video that presents the strengths of our ministries. Because the videos are mass-produced, we can afford to let the prospect keep the tape. In a visually oriented culture, many people will *watch* a brief video when they would never *read* a brochure. Our outreach teams are proud to deliver packets filled with a variety of professionally produced promotional materials.

Outreach in the local church need no longer be considered a dreaded task, performed by only the "faithful few"—those willing to go out and drag people into the Kingdom as if they were selling vacuum cleaners door to door. Instead, outreach in the local church must be viewed as every member's privilege and obligation. Christ calls all his disciples to be fishers of men. A positive outreach program is merely the extension of a life of discipleship. True disciples are always making new disciples.

Meet specific needs.

No single outreach approach is appropriate for every congregation. Communities differ, and congregations within communities differ. As a pastor and staff design an outreach program for their own church and community, they must tailor their approach to meet their own special needs. For example, in some parts of the country, a drop-by visit would be considered completely inappropriate and almost impossible to achieve because of security measures and cultural taboos. In the Sunbelt, however, a front porch visit is still an acceptable way of reaching out. Successful outreach programs will not ask members to engage in activities that make them feel uncomfortable. Outreach will be effective only when the members are well-trained, relaxed, and feel positive about the task.

As a program is established to reach out to newcomers and visitors, the church must not forget the vast resource of absentees. Most people, despite what is often believed, like to be missed when they are absent from church. A friendly phone call that communicates they were truly missed is usually received very well.

Provide multiple opportunities.

Multiple points of entry make a church more accessible to the community. Special concerts, holiday celebrations, fall festivals, and softball leagues are all possible ways of obtaining prospect names. The more exposure your church has to potential members, the more apt people will be to consider your church a desirable place of worship. Sunday morning Bible study, choir, children's programs, and singles' activities are all doors that lead to being part of your congregation.

The Sunday morning Bible study hour is no longer the main entry point into a congregation. In fact, many people visit worship several weeks before they ever dare to enter into the small group setting. Therefore, churches that seek to be successful at outreach must find new and creative doors that allow people to become a part of the church family. Divorce recovery seminars, marriage enrichment retreats, and Christian-based weight loss programs are but a few of the ways people can enter into a congregation. These activities appear less threatening than Sunday events and may, therefore, attract a whole new set of prospects.

Conclusion

An effective outreach program is a necessary ministry for a church that seeks to fulfill the Great Commission. As God's people, we are to be busy going into the community and making disciples. An outreach program will be successful when it is based upon realistic expectations, manageable assignments, the pastor's priority, and a non-confrontational approach.

Note

[1]The pastor at West Jackson has summarized his outreach program in Jerry N. Tidwell, *Outreach Teams That Win: G.R.O.W.* (Nashville: Convention Press, 1998).

Recognize children and youth as decision makers.

The decision-making power of children has been noted by Wall Street. David Leonhardt and Kathleen Kerwin wrote in *Business Week*,

> Kids are making shopping decisions once left to mom. Combining allowance, earnings, and gifts, kids fourteen and under will directly spend an estimated $20 billion this year, and they will influence another $200 billion.[1]

While marketers were once content to influence children's decisions on cereal, candy, and toy purchases, today they push computers, airline tickets, hotel accommodations, and bank services. Stein Roe and Farnham Inc., a Chicago money-management firm, runs a mutual fund for child investors consisting largely of favorites such as Disney and Nike, Inc.[2]

David Siegel, general manager of Small Talk (the division of Sive/Young and Rubicam that helps marketers reach kids), drew the same conclusion about the new family decision-making process that I have detected in church selection when he wrote, "Kids are [now] the main decision makers."[3] If current trends continue, by the year 2000, one in six Americans will be under the age of twelve.[4] Recent research in the United States, France, Germany, China, and Japan has determined that children have far more influence over family decisions than ever before.[5] Toper Taylor, senior vice president for Nelvana, a studio that specializes in children's animation, asserted that "even car companies are advertising at kids because they influence their parents' purchases."[6] James McNeal, a marketing professor at Texas A&M University who has studied children's spending patterns for thirty years, went so far as to say, "There's not a good consumer goods marketer out there that doesn't address children as either a current or potential future market."[7] Siegel added that children are not naïve victims of the marketing blitz directed their way. Rather, kids are often more discriminating in their choices than many adults.[8]

Recognizing children and youth as decision makers may be the most powerful principle of all for young families. Remember, I'm not describing the way things ought to be; I'm simply describing the way things are. More families select their church based upon the desires and wishes of their children than on any other determining factor—even more than theological concerns. While this is a poor prioritizing of the selection criteria, it is a reality churches must address. Congregations desiring to grow must recognize the power of children as decision makers and design their ministries in such a way that preschool, children, and youth programs are top priorities. These programs should have outstanding staff, facilities, and budget support in order to attract new families to the church.

Make preschoolers a priority.

Parents want to place their preschool children in facilities that appear to be safe, clean, and well managed. Small, dark, dated, and dingy facilities will send parents packing. At First Baptist Church of Amarillo, we try to do everything possible to convince parents that their preschoolers will receive the very best care. This process begins with television spots, directed toward prospective families, that highlight our spacious preschool facilities, special preschool programs, and outstanding preschool personnel.

Upon entering our preschool area, visiting families are greeted by our minister to preschoolers, Elaine Clark, an extremely dynamic, loving, and outgoing young mother who connects heart to heart with anxious parents. She quickly focuses her attention not only on the parents but also on the children, revealing a genuine interest in preschoolers. The parents are escorted to one of twenty different preschool rooms where they are introduced to caring and friendly teachers. They register their children and receive security tags that correspond to matching tags clipped to their children's clothing. The tag system communicates a sense of security and accountability because a child may be removed from the nursery only by someone with the correct security tag.

Following the assignment of the security tag, anxious parents are offered vibrating pagers. They are assured that should their children become unduly distressed or should we need them for any reason, the pagers will be activated while they are in the worship service or their own Bible study classes. Parents have the comfort, therefore, of feeling as though they are always in touch with the needs of their preschool children. They no longer have to sit and ponder, "Did he ever stop crying?"

When parents return to pick up their preschooler, Elaine and her workers describe all of the various preschool programs available at First Baptist Church: Mother's Day Out, Parent's Night Out, Day School, Summer Fun Daze, Cherub Choirs, and Mission Friends—to mention a few. Parents quickly discover that preschoolers are a priority at First Baptist Church.

Many of our best Sunday School workers are assigned to the preschool and children's areas. Our preschool and children's ministers carefully select their workers based upon their reliability, their gifts for working with children, and the good impression they will create for parents.

Commit to children's work.

The children's division must communicate a sense of excitement and fun. Dated facilities will never accomplish this task.

We recently secured the services of a leading interior designer in our city to brighten up our children's departments. Facilities more than sixty years old are now as appealing as the newest church plant in town. We used vivid primary colors, eye-catching carpet cut-outs, playful borders, and a programmatic design to transform our children's departments into the envy of any children's wing in a new hospital facility. Our updated image communicates our commitment to parents and their children. Linda Dudley, our minister to children, demonstrates a sincere interest in each child and his family. Her servant's spirit and can-do attitude create a sense of excitement within her departments.

A church without preschoolers and children is a church without a future. In a sense, they are the most important members of the congregation. Recognizing children and youth as decision makers means providing them with the very best staff, facilities, and budget support available.

Include all youth.

Relationships are the primary influences on a teenager's selection of a church. Teenagers want to go to church where their friends go. I have seen families literally change denominations in order to accommodate the desire of their child to be with her peers.

Churches that want to become regional in their impact must be able to transcend the "single high school identity." If all of the families in your church have their children enrolled in the same high school, then you can rule out attracting families who have youth attending any other high school. The youth minister and workers must make a conscious effort to be inclusive of all the schools that might be represented within the youth group. Even if only one or two of the youth attend a particular high school, the youth minister and youth department volunteers should attend the sporting events and be familiar with the student life of that campus. All area high schools must be given equal attention.

Youth facilities ought to be high tech. Our youth minister, Don Vanderslice, was having a difficult time attending all the opening assemblies of his six different youth departments—he had to be in six different places at one time. Therefore, he equipped each classroom with ceiling-mounted televisions that were interfaced with a video camera and videotape player in the youth minister's office. On Sunday mornings the youth arrive to the sounds and sights of contemporary Christian videos. Don can also, via his office camera, give the announcements simultaneously to all youth departments. He has also purchased editing equipment that allows him to exercise a great deal of creativity with his promotional videos.

Involve staff.

In October 1998, under the direction of our minister to preschoolers, Elaine Clark, our church had the highest preschool attendance in a decade. The average attendance in our preschool departments grew 20-25% in the first year of Elaine's tenure, primarily as a result of her leadership with volunteer workers. Especially within the area of preschool and children's ministry, the best staff members are often *not* those who have received formal education at a seminary. Many married women have an interest in these areas of ministry, but it is difficult to find seminary-trained preschool and children's ministers who are able to relocate their families in order to serve in a particular congregation. As Russell H. Conwell discovered, "There are acres of diamonds in your own backyard."[9]

We have recruited very capable and enthusiastic preschool and children's ministers from within our own congregation. While they do not have formal training, they have an incredible work ethic, years of good rapport with the people, and a willingness to attend seminars for professional development. Outstanding laypersons who are familiar with your congregation and your city and who have faced the complexities of parenting are able to begin meeting the needs and desires of your congregation's young families immediately. Indeed, the best staff members might already be "in your own backyard."

Provide first-class facilities.

At Meadowbrook Baptist Church we had the task of adding education space. While some of the church's leadership wanted to add an adult educational facility, I lobbied for new preschool and children's departments. Even as a church that averaged about 400 in Sunday School, we were able to design attractive and impressive preschool and children's space comparable to the best facilities in our city.

While we didn't have as many classrooms as the larger churches, the classrooms we constructed were state-of-the-art. We had a special room, including a diaper-changing station, for nursing mothers that offered the privacy they needed to care for their babies. One-way glass in the rooms for young preschool children allowed parents to observe their toddlers at all times. We positioned a welcome center, much like one found at a hotel, at each entrance to the building so young families would be greeted immediately and registered properly. We provided resource rooms, spacious restroom facilities, puppet windows, and adequate storage. Just months earlier, the church's children's area was literally an old, single-wide trailer divided into thirds.

As a result of making the change from an inadequate facility to a state-of-the-art children's complex, this medium-sized congregation became the growth leader in the Waco Baptist Association for several years. The facility communicated that preschoolers and children were a priority.

At First Baptist Church of Amarillo, we have been able to take an even more daring step toward prioritizing our little ones. In the late 1970s the church constructed a recreation facility that included six Brunswick bowling lanes. The bowling facility, over the years, became a maintenance challenge and, thus, a seldom-used portion of an otherwise outstanding recreational facility.

Recently the Family Life Center committee developed a proposal to replace the six bowling lanes with a Family Recreation Center. Under this proposal the bowling lanes disappeared, and a children's indoor, soft playground emerged. Brightly colored slides, suspension bridges, trolleys, playhouses, moon bouncers, and crawl-through tubes—much like one would find in a children's restaurant play area—have all been included. We have provided our families with recreational facilities designed to strengthen their relationships; parents and grandparents can play in the indoor park with their children or grandchildren. For fitness purposes, an adjacent aerobic exercise equipment room has been constructed. A glass wall allows parents to observe their children playing in the Family Recreation Center while they walk on treadmills, ride bicycles, or climb stairmasters.

Another aspect of this programming and facility change is that many children's birthday parties, once celebrated at the local pizza parlors and hamburger establishments, are now being held at the Family Recreation Center. We provide a specially designed party room, a birthday cake, a helping attendant dressed as a clown, and games galore at about one-third the cost of the commercial competitor. One of the greatest benefits is that the children of our congregation invite their friends to come to First Baptist Church to participate in their birthday parties. While we are not aware of any other churches making family recreation such a priority, we think it will be an effective decision.

Conclusion

Our church has realized that preschoolers, children, and youth are often the real decision makers within the family. Do not make the mistake, however, of concluding that parents only want playgrounds and parties, videos and volleyball. Parents seek churches that will allow their children to grow in mission-mindedness and service in the name of Christ. The same youth group that takes an adventure trip to a theme park must also take a mission trip to an inner city community to conduct Bible School for children who might otherwise never attend a church activity. Although we need to recognize our young people as decision makers, we must not raise a selfish generation that simply asks, "What can the church do for me?" We must make a conscious effort, in the midst of all the focus upon our young ones, to teach them the servant's heart of Christ.

Church attendance is extremely important in a child's formative years. Even Elizabeth Achtemeier, a well-known religious scholar, realized that her attendance at worship every Sunday as a child was the foundation for her present theology. She wrote,

> I did not know at the time that all those experiences were sinking into my bones—that I was learning the language of prayer and hymnody, of doctrine, scripture, and liturgy. But I was. I was slowly but surely being taught the language and worldview of the Christian faith which has nourished me all my life long.[10]

Notes

[1]David Leonhardt and Kathleen Kerwin, "Hey Kid, Buy This," *Business Week* (30 June 1997): 62.

[2]Ibid., 65. See also Nancy Coltun Webster, "Marketing to Kids," *Advertising Age* 66/7 (2 February 1995): S1-S2.

[3]Shelly Reese, "KIDMONEY: Children as Big Business," *Arts Education Policy Review* 99/3 (January/February 1998): 37. For a study that tries to delineate children's influence in decision making according to family types (autocratic, tactical, easygoing, or malleable) and personalities within families (intellectual, direct, emotional, and affable), see <http://www.good-business-sense.com/childrens-study-body.htm>.

[4]Ibid., 37.

[5]Caroline Marshall, "Protect the Parents," *Management Today* (September 1997): 92.

[6]Bill Crowe, "Advertisers See Big Buys in Little Eyes," *Broadcasting & Cable* 12/31 (28 July 1997): 47.

[7]Reese, 38.

[8]Ibid. For an interview with Sue Dibb, Co-Director of the Food Commission, which raises concerns about marketing directed at children, see <http://www.spanner.org/mclibel/interviews/dibb_sue.html>. Sue argues that McDonald's is exploiting children by their marketing efforts.

[9]Russell H. Conwell, *Acres of Diamonds* (New York: Harper & Brothers, 1915) 8-9. Conwell recounts the story told to him by an old Arab guide of the Tigris and Euphrates Rivers. In the story, Ali Hafed searches for diamonds all over the world. His search leaves him in wretchedness and poverty. At last it was discovered that while he searched fruitlessly all over the world, his own farm was in reality "the most magnificent diamond-mine in all the history of mankind." The guide advised, "Had Ali Hafed remained at home and dug his own cellar . . . or his own garden, instead of wretchedness, starvation, and death by suicide in a strange land, he would have had 'acres of diamonds.' For every acre of that old farm, yes, every shovelful, afterward revealed gems which since have decorated the crowns of monarchs."

[10]Elizabeth Achtemeier, "An Excellent Woman," *The Christian Century* 110/24 (22 August–1 September 1993): 808.

Create a positive self-image.

On 20 June 1997, I was making my usual rounds at Baptist/ St. Anthony's Hospital in Amarillo, Texas, visiting ailing church members. Among the list of our church members was the name Wade Maybin,[1] a man who had visited our church the prior Sunday. His recovery from a recent surgery was well underway, and he recognized me, thanking me for my visit. "I have to tell you," he said, "about fifteen people told me that I needed to visit First Baptist Church." Upon moving to Amarillo, Wade discovered in business encounter after business encounter that the message to newcomers was the same: "First Baptist Church is a great church, well worth your consideration." Somehow that recommendation emerged as a part of many of his conversations.

Of course, I was delighted to hear the kind words from this unbiased new resident in our community. Only a few years earlier, First Baptist's long-standing, distinguished image had been terribly tarnished. The former pastor and Baptist statesman, Dr. Winfred Moore, was no longer at the helm of the church, and the loss of his three decades of able leadership left a tremendous vacuum of vision and congregational self-esteem. Generational divisions, a short-tenured successor, and low morale had become fixtures of the landscape that saw waves of members leaving this wounded body of Christ. The community image of First Baptist Church of Amarillo was much like that of a museum—located downtown, traditional, inflexible, and focused on the great days and events of the past. Quite frankly, despite the presence of wonderful people, adequate resources, and a distinguished history, First Baptist had a self-esteem problem as a congregation and an image problem within the community of Amarillo.

The congregation I previously served, Meadowbrook Baptist Church in Waco, Texas, had been fortunate enough during its brief history to escape the negativity that surrounded the situation at First Baptist Church, Amarillo. Meadowbrook, however, suffered from anonymity within the community. As a doctoral student at Baylor University, I had lived within eight miles of Meadowbrook Baptist Church and had never heard even the mention of the congregation's existence. While looking for a church home as a seminary graduate, I had intentionally inquired about various Baptist communities of faith within the city of Waco. No one ever mentioned Meadowbrook.

How does a pastor deal with a negative or neutral community perception? How does one build the self-esteem of a congregation? How important is a positive self-image within the congregation to vital church growth?

Absolutely nothing is more important for church growth than a positive self-image in the church. A growing church, beginning with the pastor and flowing out to the congregation, should exude a sense of excitement and expectation. I was never taught this principle of church growth in seminary. In fact, I do not remember the topic being mentioned. The positive self-image principle, nonetheless, is the single most important factor for generating growth within a body of faith.

I learned this principle from Dr. Jerry Tidwell, now pastor of West Jackson Baptist Church in Jackson, Tennessee. During my tenure at Southwestern Baptist Theological Seminary, Jerry asked me to serve as the minister of youth at Garner Baptist Church where he was the pastor. Garner was a very small congregation with about forty persons participating in weekly Bible study. I told Jerry that I would simply come and visit the church one Sunday to determine whether I would have any interest in the position that he had so kindly offered. So Lisa, my wife, and I drove past Weatherford, Texas, to a small community located near Mineral Wells.

The community boasted of one service station/food mart combination and three Baptist churches. Not a single stop light interrupted the continuous landscape. The parsonage consisted of an adequate, but humble, double wide trailer, while the church building resembled the "cookie cutter" architectural layout of so many "first unit" Baptist churches built by volunteers. The driveway was gravel, with no parking spaces marked. I did not have to be inside Garner Baptist Church long, however, before I discovered that this small congregation had a very *big* self-esteem. The people were friendly, assertive, and, most of all, happy.

Jerry approached the pulpit as if he were at the helm of one of the distinguished congregations of America. His whole sermon, though I cannot remember a bit of the content, was permeated by the message that Garner was a great church with a promising future, and he was fortunate to be its pastor. His enthusiasm and excitement had been "caught" by the congregation, and I was already coming down with a bad case myself. Hearing Jerry Tidwell preach at Garner to a congregation that had consisted of only eight Sunday School attenders when he first arrived created a sense of expectation and energy. After catching Jerry's enthusiasm, the church literally thought of itself as one of the outstanding congregations in the Southern Baptist Convention. To tell the truth, I think they were right. The pastor's sincere hope and genuine love for the congregation had been infectious.

Over the years I have watched Jerry triple the attendance of three congregations, and the fourth is well underway. I certainly do not know to what Jerry would attribute the growth in those congregations, but I attribute it to his ability to create a positive self-esteem within each community of faith. Far too many pastors spend their time dreaming about service in their next congregation, failing to focus on and be excited about where God has placed them at the present.

This positive self-image is made possible when the pastor and staff show energy, enthusiasm, and a positive outlook for the future of the church. They must set the tone. As members of the congregation catch the excitement, they begin to feel good about who they are and what they are doing. Their excitement for their church becomes evident to family, friends, and co-workers, communicating the message to the surrounding community: "Come be a part of our great church." As the old adage goes, "Where there is smoke, people will seek the fire."

Promote a positive outlook.

A church's self-esteem will never rise above the pastor's projection. When everyone else sees lemons, the pastor must see lemonade. When everyone else sees insurmountable problems, the pastor must see opportunities for improvement. On 20 October 1996, the upstart Carolina Panthers remained unbeaten at home as they defeated the New Orleans Saints, 19 to 7. "We got our [rears] kicked. We couldn't do [anything]. We could not run the ball. We could not complete a pass," said Saints coach Jim Mora. "It was an awful performance. I am embarrassed and ashamed of our team. We could not stop them, and we could not move the ball. They blocked better; they were tougher; and they were coached better." "We were terrible, absolutely terrible," Mora said. "It was an embarrassing . . . playing performance by the New Orleans Saints." Mora continued with a profanity-laced tirade at his post-game news conference before stomping away from the podium and kicking open the door on his way out of the interview room. "I couldn't be more upset, and those players in there ought to be upset," Mora said.[2]

The coach must believe in himself and in his players. Mora resigned the next day. After such a demeaning tirade, it was clear to him and to the organization that the players would never be able to perform for him again. When the coach feels defeated, the team never stands a chance to win.

Unlike Mora, the pastor must be a person of hope and enthusiasm. Every community of faith will face obstacles, disappointments, and setbacks. Successful staff members will move to other congregations; offerings will fall short of budget needs; a key family will transfer its membership to "the other church" in town; or the congregation will corporately mourn the death of a child. Every congregation will face all of these challenges and many more.

The pastor's response will set the tone for the congregational response. If the pastor is publicly defeated, bitter, disappointed, or depressed, the congregation will mirror his feelings. While the pastor must be "real" and never seem aloof, his humanity must never allow him to publicly display a despondent negativity. While genuine belief in the congregation, a staff member, or a program cannot be manufactured, the pastor can begin to find more and more pieces to his congregational puzzle that he can align in a promising pattern.

Does your congregation know that you enjoy being its pastor? Do your people recognize that you believe in them? In the summer of 1984 I applied to be a lifeguard at a swim and racquet club. As the interview progressed, I realized I was actually being interviewed to manage the entire facility, not simply to sit in the sun. In such a position, I would be in charge of hiring a staff, collecting dues from members, chemically balancing two swimming pools totaling more than 200,000 gallons of water, and writing an operations manual for the facility. I was twenty-one years old and had never been in charge of a bird bath, much less a junior-sized Olympic swimming pool. As I expressed my reservations, the bank vice president who interviewed me said, "Howie, I believe you are a quick study. I believe you can do it. You're hired!"

Upon later reflection, I think the busy bank executive had been turned down by his first choice and simply selected a résumé with a good grade point average as his second choice. He had a spot to fill. Entering the room hoping to be hired to sit in the sun, soak rays, and save sinking swimmers, I left the room as manager of two large community recreational facilities —overwhelmed and anxious. Since he believed in me, however, I began to believe in myself. I poured myself into the task, working night and day until we finally transformed the amphibian-plagued ponds into crystal-clear Caribbeans. I was completely unprepared for the task. Nonetheless, the bank official's confidence in me pushed me to live up to his expectations. Similarly, a pastor must believe in the people of the church, both individually and corporately. If the congregation is ever to be excited about itself or about its future in ministry, then the pastor must set the pace. Enthusiasm is contagious.

When, at twenty-three years of age, Don Vanderslice became the minister to youth at First Baptist Church, Amarillo, he gave an acceptance speech to the congregation as it greeted him with a standing ovation. At his young age, holding a key ministerial position in such a sizable congregation was novel, to be sure. He was a bit nervous and used the word "excited" about seven times in his speech. "Well," he concluded, as he realized that his nervous energy had betrayed him into babbling just a bit, "you can tell I'm *excited*!" As pastor, I just grinned. Despite the bit of redundancy created by nervousness, Don had delivered the single most important message the congregation needed to hear: "I'm *excited* about the church, its youth ministry, and our future together." Enthusiasm, for Don, has been contagious. The youth division has grown spiritually and numerically under Don's positive "and exciting" style of leadership.

Convey external and internal enthusiasm.

External media can help foster community enthusiasm for a congregation. Television and radio spots, newspaper advertisements, and outdoor promotions are effective if they reflect genuine "in-house" enthusiasm.[3] During my tenure at Meadowbrook Baptist Church (budget $300,000) and at First Baptist Church of Amarillo (budget $3,800,000), we have utilized television commercials to draw the community's attention to our community of faith. With the advent of cable television, promotional spots have been drastically reduced in price. For example, we currently run 500 advertisements each month on popular cable channels such as *Nickelodeon, ESPN,* or the *Weather Channel* for only $2 each. Your local cable company, moreover, can produce a 30-second spot for about $200, while high-quality professional work can be "voiced over" for your church for about $2,000.

While the technical superiority of the professionally produced spot is clearly evident, many churches prefer the personal appeal of locally produced promotions. Careful planning and preparation, along with simplicity, can yield locally produced spots that do not appear to be from the genre of the "used car lot" advertisements. Our members prefer to see our own children over polished child actors and their own pastor over a more professional, but unknown, generic spokesman.

Outdoor promotions can also supplement genuine "in-house" enthusiasm. The price of a billboard depends on its size, location (traffic count), and illumination. Small billboards may be priced as low as $70 per month, while interstate readable signage may cost several thousand dollars each month. Billboards offer an excellent opportunity for the church to deliver images and messages to multitudes who will never enter a sanctuary. Promoting a clear gospel message rather than an oversized picture of the megalomaniacal pastor is the best use of outdoor signage for the congregation concerned with integrity. Traditional congregations should *not* shy away from billboards as something crassly commercial simply because other congregations have employed them in a less than authentic manner. The billboard is simply a vehicle and is not intrinsically appropriate or inappropriate for building a church's self-esteem.

Radio is another effective medium for churches. Begin by asking the question: "What station do most of our members listen to?" Only after knowing the musical preferences of your present congregation can you realistically determine which stations would be best suited to reach your target market.[4] One friend of mine uses the title "Sixty Golden Seconds" to deliver a daily radio message to the people of his community. By combining the promotional information about his church (including name, location, and other pertinent information) with an inspirational story, the radio spot is softer and more appealing than a direct advertisement.

Currently the congregation I serve uses the radio in a limited capacity. We broadcast the morning and evening Sunday services and also participate aggressively in high school football broadcasts. Local high school football games have the attention of much of the community, and supporting such community events by purchasing air time allows everyone to see the church as a local "team player" in more ways than one.

While large and colorful newspaper ads are very expensive and have only a twenty-four-hour shelf life, smaller, more frequent advertisements can be extremely effective and yet reasonably priced. For example, the *Amarillo Globe-News* uses one inch by one column "fill-in ads" throughout its publication. These small but powerful reminders usually cost only a few dollars each. Utilizing this less expensive technique, we are certain the thorough reader of the newspaper sees our name two or three times each day, depending on how space permits the "fill-ins" to be placed. Another important printed media that is handled every day by residents, especially newcomers, is the telephone book Yellow Pages. A comprehensive promotional package should include adequate Yellow Page coverage.

Many churches purchase promotional media space or time in a haphazard manner. It is better for the pastor and a committee to develop a year's comprehensive plan encompassing budgets, logos, consistent and complementary messages, and overall goals. The promotional plan should address these questions: (1) What message are we trying to communicate about our church? (2) To whom are we trying to communicate our message? (3) What promotional channels will be most cost effective to accomplish our goals?

It is extremely important to remember, however, that external media are only effective when there is a genuine spirit of enthusiasm and excitement within the congregation. Stated simply, there must be truth behind your promotional messages.

In most smaller and medium-sized towns, churches have the potential of free advertising through newspaper and television special interest stories. Every congregation should keep handy a list of the appropriate contact people at the newspaper and the facsimile numbers of newspaper and television stations for press releases.

We often invite personalities from our local newspaper and television stations to attend special events at our church. For example, in June 1998 representatives from the newspaper and one of the television stations attended and photographed our First Family Fun Day, a carnival promoted by our minister of recreation. On the Sunday following First Family Fun Day, we had a photograph in the newspaper and about twenty seconds on the evening news picturing happy families at First Baptist Church. The market value of those two promotions would total about $600 to $700. By planning ahead and developing a good relationship with the local personnel of television stations and newspapers, your church can benefit from free promotional time and space.

Incorporate the promotional power of people.

Having more power than the promotional punch of television, radio, and newspapers combined, church members are your greatest marketing asset or liability. Members always share their feelings about their church with their neighbors, co-workers, and friends. Unfortunately, this is especially true when those perceptions are negative. Therefore, any real attempt to "heal" a church must begin with creating healthy attitudes within the existing church family. Positive images from external media will be more than nullified by one negative comment made by a carping church attender. Enthusiastic comments from approving members, however, are your most effective way of building a positive community image. A growing church must have a positive self-image that creates a positive community perception.

All churches have a community image. Every church in every city is labeled by its community. The community sees each church as growing or declining, friendly or stilted, relevant or irrelevant, effective or ineffective, and harmonious or divisive. While small pockets of misinformation exist about every community of faith, the comprehensive community assessment seldom exists without substantial truth.

Before you decide to serve in a particular church, randomly interview community members to determine the community's perception of the congregation. One search committee that was considering me to be their pastor went beyond the formal reference checks by scouring the community in search of tidbits of information. They were seen in a convenience store, the local restaurants, and similar community institutions, casually inquiring, "What do you know about the pastor of Meadowbrook?" One wise friend commented, "Pastor, they have thoroughly investigated you. Have you considered going to their city and casually investigating the community's perception of their congregation? They will know who you are, but will you know who they are?"

Discovering the current assessment of your congregation by listening openly and nondefensively to those around you is essential before you can develop a new community image. Put simply, you have to know where you are before you can get where you are going.

Members will share positive comments about their church when they hear positive comments about the congregation from the leadership. If the pastor belittles the people, the people will belittle the church. The pastor and staff must speak positively about the future of the ministries of the church. First Baptist Church of Amarillo has been a large congregation for decades. In 1945, 3,056 people attended the church Sunday School on high attendance day. The distinguished list of previous pastors includes a seminary president, J. Howard Williams; a Southern Baptist Convention president, Carl E. Bates; and Baptist General Convention of Texas president and Southern Baptist Convention vice-president, Winfred Moore. If any congregation ever had justification to look back, to praise the "good old days," and to despair the future, First Baptist Church of Amarillo would be that congregation.

When I fearfully and unexpectedly became the pastor at thirty-two years of age, however, I praised the church's great heritage but insisted that the greatest days were to be found "looking through the front windshield and not in the rearview mirror." The best is yet to come. I communicate to the people that I believe in them and know God has great plans for their future as a church. Because I am optimistic, they are optimistic. The pastor's excitement is caught by the staff, and the staff's enthusiasm is caught by the people.

Far too many pastors deliver a eulogy for their congregation in each week's sermon. Their subtle negativity portrays their hopelessness for the church's future. If the people are scolded and belittled week after week, we can be certain they will not invite their friends to "come worship with us!"

Build on strengths.

Focus on your strengths. Pick out three things the church is doing well and draw attention to the strengths of these ministries. Despite the fact that the preschool ceiling leaks over the baby cribs, or the choir's anthem is a half step off key, or the church van has no air conditioning, or the sanctuary sound system pops like firecrackers on the Fourth of July, every church has some strengths.

Perhaps your church has built a strong in-home ministry or an extensive ministry to nursing homes. Children's church might be the focal point around which you can begin to offer praise to the congregation. As you highlight the vitality and results from your strongest areas of ministry, other areas of ministry also begin to improve.

Likewise, if the pastor continually harps and criticizes, he will eventually demoralize his people. Many ministries exist within your congregation that people have taken for granted or ignored. For example, First Baptist Church of Amarillo operates Buchanan Street Chapel, which includes a food pantry, clothes closet, and fully functioning congregation just a few blocks away from our main campus. Many members did not even realize this benevolent work was part of the ministry of their church despite the enormity of the operation. Since the ministry's inception in 1989, more than 27,000 people have received help through this ministry. One particular lady has handsewn 575 quilts over that time span and given them to warm the needy. While our congregation was doing much to help meet the basic needs in our community, our people were pining that we were doing nothing. Lack of information about a vital ministry was a barrier to a positive attitude about our benevolence ministries.

Improve on weaknesses.

Demonstrate real improvements in areas of weakness. While the best starting point is to highlight and praise some successful ministries already existing in your congregation, equally important is an honest assessment of ministries that need improvement. Every growing and changing congregation must constantly evaluate its various ministries. Does the ministry still meet the needs of people in the congregation or community? Is the ministry just an antique from the glorious past being tightly clutched by the congregation? Are there some specific steps that can be taken to improve the personnel and programming of the ministry? Church members begin to feel good about themselves as they see marked improvement in an area heretofore seen as a weakness.

For example, First Baptist Church of Amarillo was involving only twenty people in its outreach program on Tuesday evenings. Despite the fact that the ministry was publicized, announced during the worship services, and proclaimed from the pulpit, the interest was nonexistent. Once logical and proper steps were taken, the church outreach program grew within a year to include about 400 persons each month, with a weekly average attendance of 100 persons reaching out to our community. This success was made possible because of several factors:

- We acknowledged that the present program was ineffective.
- We studied other congregations who were having success with outreach, observing the sources of their effectiveness.
- We went to our people and reaffirmed our commitment to reaching out to our community with this new plan.

• The new ministry was not simply the old ministry with a new façade.

Every pastor will soon learn that however much he would like to spend all of his time studying for the proclamation of the word, one of his main tasks is in the area of troubleshooting. He must ask himself, "Where are we weak? How can we improve?"

Another example of weakness was the summer programming for children at a church I previously served. After our usual mission studies were dismissed for the summer, we found almost no attendance in our children's activities on Wednesday evenings. Once again, we acknowledged the failure of our current program, envisioned and brainstormed a new concept of ministry, and soon, Wednesday evening children's activities were the highlight of the church week. Prior to our reevaluation, we could find no one to volunteer for children's activities in the summer. Following our recommitment and reevaluation, almost all of our committed church families wanted to be involved on Wednesday nights.

A congregation must see the pastor and staff as responsive and proactive in making improvements and changes. Once a congregation begins to feel as if the status quo will never be changed, as if their complaints go unheard, or as if weaknesses are simply swept under the rug, then the congregation begins to have a lethargic attitude about their pastor, staff, and the ministries of the church as a whole.

Sometimes changes are simple. For example, at First Amarillo our Sunday evening radio broadcast left much to be desired. Some weeks the signal was strong and clear. Other weeks we were preempted by the static from other stations. Our people had just become accustomed to not knowing whether they were going to be able to hear our broadcasts in the evenings. Week after week the same people would call, saying their complaints were going unheeded. After several attempts to get our current radio station to address the problem, we finally turned to a new station, changing from AM to FM and providing our membership with a powerful, clear signal during each broadcast. What had once been a symbol of inefficiency and acceptance of mediocrity had become a symbol of change, improvement, and clarity.

As the congregation experiences improvements, it begins to realize that change is possible, progress is probable, and the church is on the move. As a word of caution, however, realize as you begin to make improvements to the ministries and environment of your church, people will think of many more things that "we should be doing" to make improvements. The pastor, staff, and church leadership will face the challenge of making some marked and steady improvements without, however, accepting every suggestion that is offered.

A church should not, moreover, begin a ministry or continue a ministry it cannot do with excellence. It is better for a congregation to commit itself to doing fewer things well than to doing many things poorly. For example, your congregation may or may not want to have a counseling ministry. If your congregation does provide a counseling ministry, it should be conducted by trained professionals. It is better for a congregation to make referrals to a local Christian counselor than to attempt to undertake a task beyond its means. Meeting people's emotional, spiritual, and psychological needs through counseling is too important to approach haphazardly. Many congregations begin ministries before they really count the cost of the long-term burden of carrying that ministry forward for years to come.

Conclusion

The growing church possesses a sense of excitement and expectation. The pastor and staff must embody this enthusiasm. As the pastor and people celebrate their strengths and evaluate and improve their weaknesses, the church develops a positive self-image. While external media serve as supplemental promotional tools, a positive remark from a church member is the most effective method of creating community interest in the congregation.

Congregations can be either the greatest catalyst or worst hindrance to their own growth. As the congregation emits positive messages, visitors are drawn to the healthy body of Christ. Conversely, negative messages warn would-be visitors to stay away from a weak and ailing body of believers. The ability to create a positive self-image must begin with the pastor and flow out to the members. I have never seen a congregation with a poor self-image that was able to foster growth.

Notes

[1] Name changed.

[2] "New Orleans vs. Carolina," in *USA Today*, 21 October 1996, <http://usatoday.com/sports/scores96/96294/96294319.htm>. "Panthers 19, Saints 7," in *Lexington Herald Leader*, 21 October 1996, <http://www.kentuckyconnect.com/heraldleader/news/1021/fs21nfc.htm>. "Johnson Sparkles for Carolina," *The Augusta Chronicle*, 21 October 1996, http://www.augustachronicle.com/headlines/102196/carolina_saints.htm.

[3] While I am encouraging the use of various media to generate community interest in the church, I am not endorsing a marketing approach to sharing the gospel. We should not treat the unchurched as potential consumers. As Christopher Lasch noted, consumers are "perpetually unsatisfied, restless, anxious, and bored." We cannot be just another option to cure the discontentment of a self-centered society. We cannot be in the business of satisfying the "felt needs" of religious consumers. See Christopher Lasch, *The Culture of Narcissism* (New York: W. W. Norton, 1979) 72. See also Douglas Webster, *Selling Jesus: What's Wrong with Marketing the Church* (Downers Grove IL: Intervarsity Press, 1992).

[4] This, of course, assumes that your target market shares the same demographic profile as your current membership.

Provide church plant support.

As an aquarium enthusiast, I often visit Bubbles, a fresh and salt water pet store in Amarillo, Texas. On one visit I noticed an Oscar fish that was short in length and unusually stocky. His body shape was, quite frankly, odd. It looked as if his insides had kept growing while his outside had tried to remain small. I couldn't help but inquire about the unusual fish. "Is this a new breed of Oscar?" I asked. "Oh no," replied the attendant, "his growth was stunted because he spent years in a tank that was just too small."

Many churches are like that Oscar fish. They try to fit more and more people into small, inadequate, and outdated facilities. Nothing will halt growth more quickly than facilities that are already "maxed out." Some churches, despite the fact they are already filled to capacity, continue to attract new members. Their average weekly attendance, however, never increases. Imagine a rain barrel full and overflowing. As additional drops plunge into the barrel, they simply displace other drops that are forced to run over the side. Like the overflowing rain barrel, the church that does not provide adequate facilities to attract and retain new members will find itself stagnant. In fact, it has been observed that educational and worship facilities are governed by an invisible "80% rule." This rule suggests that new visitors do not feel comfortable if the room is more than 80% full. Chairs lined around the perimeter of the sanctuary communicate that there is no room for newcomers.[1]

At Meadowbrook Baptist Church I found inadequate church facilities to be the single greatest barrier to growth. The excitement of finding a new pastor and staff created a great deal of growth in our average Sunday School attendance (19%) my first year, but we plateaued very quickly the second year, increasing our average Sunday School attendance by only four people (1%).[2] The dilemma was clear: all the excitement in the world would not be able to foster growth until we solved our space problem. Three of our children's departments were housed in one single-wide trailer. Preschoolers were packed into small and inadequate rooms. Senior adults were sitting closer together than twenty-six circus clowns in a Volkswagon Beetle. At the same time, though, our college department had ten times more space than was required for its attendance. The addition of new facilities and the adequate management of existing facilities are necessary in order to maximize church growth. Utilizing both factors, Meadowbrook was able to obtain 50% growth in average Sunday School attendance within four years.

Utilize existing space.

Before a congregation attempts to accelerate its growth by constructing new facilities, it should make certain that existing facilities are being properly utilized. While Meadowbrook's large senior adult department was crammed into its smallest assembly room, the small college department was meeting in an enormous space. Of course, land mines may be tripped if people are moved from *their* Sunday School room! This territorial tendency seems to be especially associated with those adults who hang curtains, purchase their own padded chairs, and imagine that Sunday School rooms are their property. I have found, however, that most church members are very reasonable if a thorough study is conducted, and the results are clearly communicated.

Many existing books explain the square footage requirements for Bible study based upon the age classification of the department.[3] Preschoolers, of course, need the most space per capita (25-35 square feet), and adults need the least (10-12 square feet). Using these standard formulas, a committee can conduct a space utilization study and make recommendations for improving efficiency in space management. If respected leaders from a cross-section of the congregation are included on the committee, then members of the congregation feel well represented and usually accept the results of the study with minimal resistance.

I have encountered churches that allowed their Sunday School rooms to be used by separate, but affiliated, schools. This posed a problem: the Sunday School space was really a school classroom. Flags, maps, language arts posters, and bulletin boards all created an academic atmosphere. It appeared as if Bible study was a secondary activity that just happened to take place in an elementary school classroom. Managing space for Bible study growth requires giving priority to Sunday morning classes over any other possible activities that might occur in the room! Sitting in school desks during Sunday School and fellowship time is awkward at best.

Provide temporary facilities.

"Temporary" can mean different things to different people. The "temporary trailer" at Meadowbrook Baptist Church was used for many years to house children's departments. This intended short-term solution turned into a long-term problem. First Baptist Church of Amarillo has a "temporary" singles building that has now been utilized for more than a decade. The singles often remind me of the promise that the building would only be used until a permanent, new facility could be constructed. First Baptist Church of Nederland, Texas, has housed children's Sunday School departments in a "temporary facility" for more than forty years. The children who originally met in the facility now bring their grandchildren to the same "temporary facility!" A high school I drive by every day has "temporary classrooms" that have been cluttering the landscape of the school for years. The problem with temporary is that it usually becomes permanent. A "quick fix now" might actually delay a more permanent solution to your space problems by removing the urgency to build.

I'm certainly not advocating that temporary facilities should never be utilized. In fact, those still occupied at First Baptist Church of Amarillo are of exceptional quality—equivalent to our main campus—and have offered a "short-term solution" to a "long-term problem." It is best, however, to be realistic about the number of years such facilities will be employed so the people who are using them will not be disappointed or feel misled. In fact, there is currently some discussion about adding a kitchenette to our "temporary building," which shows how permanent it really is.

Devise a master plan.

Churches that construct buildings without adequate planning are actually erecting barriers to future growth. A well-designed master plan will communicate a clear vision to the congregation and the community. Knowing where all the buildings will eventually be placed on the church property allows for a future church plant that will snap together like a jigsaw puzzle. The whole picture evolves in a logical fashion.

The tragedy of the Winchester Mansion has been repeated in many church building programs. Mrs. Winchester was convinced by a spiritualistic medium that the lives of her husband and daughter had been taken by the spirits of those who had been killed by "the gun that won the West." She was convinced she would share their fate unless she began building a mansion for the spirits, who had stipulated she would be allowed to live only as long as construction continued—uninterrupted.

With a thousand dollars a day in royalties from the Winchester Rifle fortune, Sarah Winchester ensured that the sound of the carpenter's hammer echoed 24 hours a day for almost 30 years. The racket was soul-soothing music to her ears because the construction activity kept the spirits of death at bay. The result of the construction marathon was a 160-room mansion with 47 fireplaces, 13 bathrooms, and 10,000 windows—all arranged in the most haphazard fashion. Visitors touring the mansion today should be careful: one door opens to a two-story drop awaiting unwary guests; others open into solid walls; and stairways lead to nowhere. Upon Sarah Winchester's death, it took six weeks to move the furniture out of her uncanny labyrinth because the workers were continually getting lost in the never-ending maze.[4]

Without contemplating future scenarios, many churches begin construction to meet their immediate space needs. This lack of master planning has created a multitude of church campuses that resemble the Winchester Mansion. They have dead-end stairways and narrow, winding hallways.

Failure to develop a master plan that accommodates future growth will ultimately bring the congregation's growth to a standstill or force the church to abandon the present location altogether. A church located in one of the fastest growing counties in Texas, the north Austin area, is currently having to consider a total relocation because it failed to envision future growth. The congregation will eventually have to abandon an 800-seat sanctuary and educational and recreational facilities worth millions of dollars. Another Texas church had to leave behind a 1,600-seat sanctuary because it did not plan for parking! The total relocation has created millions of dollars of debt and dissension within the congregation. The congregation, however, will avoid future disaster because they have now developed a thoughtful master plan that invites growth.

Adequate master site planning requires adequate property. Churches must consider parking needs, worship needs, educational needs, and recreational needs. A rough rule of thumb indicates the master site should provide one acre of property for every 100 attenders. Local codes and restrictions, topography, and special needs may require even more property.[5] While the 100 people per acre rule includes parking needs, churches can project that one acre will park 100 cars if no landscaping islands are used.[6] Parking space is just as important as pew space!

Master planning or phasing also gives church members the assurance that the church plant will eventually address all the needs of the church's ministries. As Robert Lowry states, "It can help relieve the anxiety a member feels because a particular facility in which he is most interested is not slated for construction next."[7] Church members want to contribute to thoughtful plans that give a sense of direction and assurance.

Employ professionals.

Choosing to employ the services of an experienced architect and interior designer might be the best decision a building committee makes. Many states or local governments, in fact, have various codes and laws requiring the services of an architectural professional for certain projects.[8] Interview several architectural firms in the selection process and visit some of their completed projects to make an assessment of their capabilities and to appreciate their individual styles. Like the artistic similarities of Vincent Van Gogh's paintings, the buildings of a single architect usually share a similar "architectural atmosphere."[9] The committee members should make certain they understand the architect's fee structure, scope of work, and key role in the implementation of a successful building or renovation project.[10] While the committee should allow the architect to offer professional advice, the committee members need to realize that they are the experts concerning how the facility will be utilized by the community of faith.

Like the architect's services, the services of an interior designer are very important. Many churches will spend $30,000 to carpet a new building but will not spend $300 to consult with an interior designer to make certain the appropriate carpet is selected. The building committee process flows more smoothly when committee members are guided by a competent professional rather than bickering over their choice of carpet color. Just as the conductor of a symphony combines a multitude of sounds into a musical masterpiece, the interior designer orchestrates various textures and colors of carpets, paints, wall coverings, fixtures, and furnishings in order to create a mood for the space.

The interior designer should always seek input from committee members because they best understand the desires of the congregation and the function of the new space. For example, we asked our interior designer at Meadowbrook to cover one-third of each of the children's rooms with a vinyl tile that complemented the carpet. The tile was selected to accommodate everything from finger painting to serving refreshments.

Build new facilities.

Contemporary thought concerning new church facilities is greatly misguided. Many writers are now telling us that churches have more financial freedom if they do not have the burden of building and maintaining large facilities. This philosophy asserts that the church is people—not bricks and mortar! In its purest form this philosophy proposes a progressive insight. The church could spend more money on missions and ministry and less on painting and plumbing. Advocates of this philosophy argue that the New Testament speaks of "house churches" and not church facility construction. In fact,

107

it is not until Constantine granted toleration to the church in the fourth century that we find significant church building activity. As McCormick noted, "Some churches are even started with the pledge that church buildings, the edifice complex, is to be avoided."[11]

While this philosophy is appealing in theory, it seldom works in practice. If the church is going to be the gathered people of God, the people must have a place to gather. They must either lease, build, or purchase a place to call their own. A church building within a community is, in itself, a witness to the gathered people of God. We have all seen postcards that depict a church nestled within a city, making a statement of the presence and importance of God within that community.

The success story of many churches, moreover, makes clear that congregations can both build needed church facilities and provide generous missionary and ministry funds. In fact, churches that avoid purchasing property and constructing facilities have *not* demonstrated patterns of giving an unusually large percentage of their total receipts to mission causes. According to a study of 9,220 Southern Baptist churches that have had consistent growth patterns, those congregations that constructed facilities during their growth period actually showed stronger mission support than churches that did not build! Churches involved in construction significantly increased their missions gifts. McCormick concluded,

> The study revealed that growing churches with a strong commitment to missions generally will increase missions giving. The increase usually will occur at a faster rate in the churches that build than it occurs in similar churches that are not in a building program.[12]

First Baptist Church of Amarillo's Missions Committee is currently considering a joint effort with a church in Uganda,

Africa, that feels as if it is hindered by its lack of adequate facilities. The Baptist Association in Apac has plans for three new buildings on its campus. The roof will possibly be made of thatch, and the bricks might consist of little more than dried mud, but the new church will stand in that community as a great testimony to the witness and work of the gospel. Whether it is the $15,000 building in Uganda or the $40 million church plant of a downtown megachurch, all churches must have culturally appropriate facilities that foster the mission and ministries of gathered believers.

While there is no doubt that church facilities are a large drain on a congregation's financial resources, those monies are well spent. Church growth occurs more readily when a church can invite the community to visit its new facilities. This is especially true in the area of preschool, children, and youth ministries. The new facility itself communicates to the community that the church is growing, reaching, and risking for the Kingdom of God.

When Meadowbrook Baptist Church opened its new Family Education Center, an addition that doubled the Bible study space, it quickly became the fastest growing church in the Waco area, winning the Waco Baptist Association's Sunday School Growth Award in 1995. Carefully planned building projects do produce growth!

Establish multiple services.

One way to double sanctuary or educational space instantly and inexpensively is to conduct multiple services. While the sanctuary at First Baptist Church of Amarillo has a seating capacity of only 1,500, our second worship service permits us to provide worship space for 3,000 people. Not only do multiple services double the seating capacity, but they also offer worshipers more options. At Meadowbrook Baptist Church the addition of an early (eight o'clock) worship service attracted some worshipers who would have never attended worship at eleven o'clock. They were attracted by plentiful parking spaces, a smaller crowd, and a long afternoon for leisure or work.

The greatest challenge for multiple worship services is developing and maintaining two choirs. Multiple Sunday Schools are even more complex because they require additional volunteer recruitment and can possibly place family members in different Bible studies or worship services. Despite the challenges, many churches have used multiple Sunday Schools very effectively.

Maintain facilities.

First impressions are powerful. Churches with poorly maintained facilities make a negative statement before the choir sings a note or the pastor utters a prophetic word.[13] Meadowbrook, for example, drastically needed remodeling. Each building was veneered in a different color and style of brick. One building was red, one was white, and one was varicolored. To make matters worse, shingle patches dotted the roof, flaking paint exposed the raw wood of the trim, and landscaping had been long neglected.

Before constructing our new education facility, we painted the brick on all existing educational buildings a uniform color, put crisp vinyl siding on the trim, covered the entire church plant with an upgraded shingle, updated and added restrooms, purchased new signage, and landscaped. In doing so, we made a positive statement to our visitors and community, and our members began to take ownership and pride in their church as a whole. In fact, I began to wonder if I had oversold my point because, once a sense of pride was established, our members demanded we do everything first-class. They were constantly looking for other ways to update and improve the facilities.

First Baptist Church of Amarillo also had portions of the church plant that made a negative first impression. Adorned with elaborate, hand-painted frescoes and breathtaking stained glass windows, the sanctuary of First Baptist Church is arguably one of the most beautiful in the entire Southern Baptist Convention. Despite this artistic excellence, however, the carpet was threadbare, the pew finishes were worn to the wood, and the sound system was eighteen years old. While visitors were impressed by the decorative, handpainted, sculptured plaster and a handpainted tile ceiling which stands a voluminous fifty-five feet high, they were also negatively impacted by peeling plaster and wooden balcony chairs with splintered veneer. The elegant grandeur of the room combined with the maintenance maladies to communicate "This *was* a great place."

First Baptist needed to take quick and drastic measures to restore its sanctuary—to communicate "This *is* a great place!" Following a restoration program that involved paint, artistic restoration, refinished pews, sculpture repair, electrical wiring, increased lighting, new audio and video equipment, new carpet, restored terrazzo, and stained glass repair, the image of the sanctuary is now overwhelmingly positive. The sanctuary alone was recently valued at more than $15,000,000.[14] The restoration of the sanctuary is symbolic of the restoration of the spirit and image of the congregation.

The children's educational wings at First Baptist Church of Amarillo were in satisfactory condition. The carpet was less than ten years old, the paint was relatively new, and everything was in good repair. The entire educational building had been carefully restored less than a decade earlier. The committee had done an excellent job laying the foundation for the educational areas. Today, however, many churches that build new educational facilities use interior design techniques with bright colors, making their children's departments very warm, exciting, and inviting.

Without any great expenditure, we were able to employ the services of an interior designer to recast the image of our children's area.[15] A thoughtful plan allowed us to build upon the foundation of the educational renovation that had taken place earlier. The existing carpet was used as a base into which primary-colored carpet art, in the shapes of circles, triangles, and squares, was inserted. Bright, eye-catching paint was applied to the walls, and playful eighteen-inch decorative borders were strategically placed for special effect. The flavor of the children's area was transformed from vanilla to tutti-frutti with candy sprinkles on top! The new design did not replace what the church had already done but, rather, added the finishing touches. As one of our first graders commented to her Sunday School teacher, "This place used to look kinda lady-ish, but now it looks kid-ish."

We are constantly in search of ways to improve the appearance of our facilities. Fresh paint and new carpet set a healthful and wholesome tone, creating confidence in the church's programs. At First Baptist Church of Amarillo, we have a painter on staff. Major hallways are painted twice each year. With more than 300,000 square feet to manage, painting is an everyday chore. The properties manager/facilities director and his maintenance and housekeeping employees are treated with the same respect as our ministerial and support staff. The endless task of keeping the facilities in impeccable condition is as important as anything we do.

Conclusion

Church plant support is essential for church growth. Churches with poorly maintained facilities, inefficient space management, and overcrowded classrooms will seldom experience growth. Congregations must employ professionals in order to develop a master plan that will serve the needs of future generations. Merely meeting current needs as cheaply and quickly as possible will only lead to disaster in the future. Many congregations meander through ill-planned mazes, stand landlocked, and ponder about parking because previous congregational leaders did not adhere to the principle of providing church plant support.

Notes

[1]Robert Lowry, *Designing Educational Buildings* (Nashville: Convention Press): 17.

[2]Average Sunday School attendance: 1991—308; 1992—365; 1993—369; 1994—413; 1995—460. See yearly annual of the Baptist General Convention of Texas (BGCT).

[3]Lowry, *Designing Educational Buildings*; T. Lee Anderson, *Church Property/Building Guidebook* (Nashville: Convention Press, 1980).

[4]*Winchester Mystery House* (Oakland CA: Mike Roberts, N.D.). See "Winchester Mystery House," <http://www.gate.met/~garlopez/winhouse.html>.

[5]Lowry, 11

[6]Anderson, 196.

[7]Lowry, 13. See also Gwenn E. McCormick, *Designing Worship Centers* (Nashville: Convention Press, 1988) 19-20.

[8]Many thanks to Dan Patterson for sharing his architectural expertise with First Baptist Church of Amarillo.

[9]McCormick, 21-25.

[10]Read the Architect's Standard Contracts carefully and consult an attorney before signing. The AIA contracts used by many architects make every effort to protect the architect's interests while leaving the owner and contractor with little protection.

[11]McCormick, 8.

[12]McCormick, 9.

[13]See Tim Holcomb, *A Maintenance Management Manual for Southern Baptist Churches*, (Nashville: Convention Press. 1990). Holcomb suggests a church should spend 4-6 percent of its budget on building maintenance and repair. See Holcomb's manual for very practical information, including generally accepted housekeeping standards.

[14]Busby & Associates Inc., Houston TX.

[15]Many thanks to Mary Stephens of Stephens & Hagan Interior Design for the generosity in donating her time to First Baptist Church of Amarillo.

Issue a clear call to commitment.

The Reverend Thaine Ford has succeeded in providing what many church members cherish most—a guarantee to get out by noon. In fact, you can be home by noon. This pastor of the First American Baptist Church of Pensacola, Florida, has created the "Compact Mini 22-Minute Worship Service." In just 1,320 seconds Ford delivers an eight-minute sermon, leads in the singing of one hymn, reads Scripture, and has a prayer. His logic is this:

> It's for people whose parents made them go to church all their lives, and they thought they had all the church they could stand. Or, it's a good entry-level church for people to see if they can take religion in smaller doses.[1]

It may be a creative way to reach the unchurched, but what kind of message does this "no-commitment" service send to the world?

Blend the old with the new.

Randall O'Brien, Baylor University religion professor, called my attention to the movement in our society toward "lite" church. It was bound to happen. Americans have had McLean hamburgers at McDonalds, Hellman's Lite Mayo, and even Braum's no-fat sundaes. It should come as no surprise that we would want "lite church" these days. A cultural phenomenon is sweeping our country. We want one-half the calories, no fat, and yet the same full, delicious taste. Likewise, we want "lite Christianity"—Christianity that has grace but no judgment, forgiveness but no repentance, church membership but no baptism, and heaven but, please, no hell. Lite church would have:

- 43% less visitation
- 24% fewer commitments
- 39% fewer tithers (home of the 5% tithe)
- 51% fewer baptisms and decisions at invitation
- 44% fewer commitments to happy marriages and homes
- 7 commandments—your choice

Tastes great! Everything you wanted in a church . . . and less.[2]

Perhaps by some accounts we've made much progress. We celebrate Christianity with a Savior but no Satan. This new brand of evangelicalism tickles the ears of modern society. We have slowly and surgically sought to sever the awful offense of the gospel. We have removed the strong call to commitment, to take up one's cross and follow the Christ.

Many of us would have concluded that evangelical Christianity, especially in its fundamentalist form, would never fail to issue a clear call to commitment to would-be disciples. What we find, ironically, is an emphasis—especially in fundamentalist churches—on doing whatever is necessary to attract new worshipers, even if the message must be diluted.[3] While this is well intentioned, we are left with a generation of babes in Christ who have never counted the cost before they followed the Christ.

I recently received literature from two evangelical churches that serve as excellent examples of promoting lite Christianity. One promotional pamphlet began with the headline, "Not Into Organized Religion? Neither Are We!" The church promised to be "always casual, always contemporary, and always laughter." The brochure proceeded to promise:

(1) We communicate in ways that work! We use drama that would make Seinfeld laugh. Our music is real jazz/rock. Hey, for Easter we performed Edgar Winter's Free Ride (yes, real Rock). Our multimedia makes "Titanic" look cheezy (well almost). (2) We don't have "sermons." We have

conversational Biblically-based teaching that is designed to give you real tools for living a real life. (3) We always finish early, so you can *get on with your day*.[4]

The second brochure I received within the same month declared that it was time for the "Top 10 Church Hassles" to be avoided by attending their church. For example, they promise:

(1) No long, boring services. We specialize in the quick 60-minute worship service. (2) No strong teaching on stewardship. At our church, "giving comes from the heart, not twisted arms." (3) No "music from the 15th Century." Our songs are "from the heart" and "make worship come alive." We offer the "hassle-free church."[5]

As I browse publications and promises such as these from evangelical churches, I ponder, "What does the brand of discipleship marketed in these pamphlets have to do with historic Christianity?"[6] These churches almost apologize for their worship, promising they will get through with the service as quickly as possible.

Lite Christianity has long forgotten historic Christianity's day of worship, a day set aside for the covenant community to gather together, sing praises to God, and hear the reading of His word. As Marva J. Dawn noted, we have allowed efficiency, an idol of our society, to invade our church and its worship. She observed that the liturgy becomes clockwork, service elements are eliminated, free expression of praise is stifled, the sermon is cut so brief that no deep biblical explication can occur, and hymn verses are chopped off.[7]

No place exists in such communities for the prophet to declare to the people, "Thus sayeth the Lord . . .," pointing directly to the social sins of humanity. In these sermon-free services God is not allowed to use the foolishness of preaching

117

the message to draw people to His kingdom. When he had an encounter with the Holy God, we can hardly imagine the ancient prophet Isaiah declaring, "Lord, let's just keep it casual, contemporary, and full of laughter."

This new brand of evangelical Christianity has so weakened the call to discipleship that church has become little more than a caring community centered around a warm pep rally. It promises never to be confrontational. The emphasis is almost exclusively on pop psychology, helping us to be "better husbands and wives," to have "success over stress," or to be "winners in the workplace"—the billboard sermon titles coming from fundamentalist Christianity. Lite Christianity rests upon theology that can fit in a thimble and uses the text as a springboard to produce practical, people-pleasing sermonettes.

Willimon recalls a psychiatrist who told a preacher friend he would go back to church only when they started talking about God again. The preacher asked the psychiatrist what they talked about when he went to church. He responded,

> Oh, I hear advice on how to be friendly, how to vote, how to have a happy marriage, and how to feel better about myself. It's all good advice, but it's not different from the advice I get anywhere else. I don't think I need more advice; certainly I don't need more information; rarely do I know what to do with more exhortation—I can't get it out of my head that I need God.[8]

Count the costs.

In Luke 14 Jesus makes it clear that we need to be people who "count the cost." Nothing is more disturbing than seeing a partially erected building relinquished to the elements or hearing of an almost completed degree abandoned just a few course hours before requirements have been met. In one South

Carolina town a church once poured a foundation and started laying blocks for the walls. But suddenly the work stopped. Until this day the grass has grown, overtaking the foundation as it sits in front of the church as a monument to someone's miscalculation.

While our humanity delights in having masses flow through the church, Jesus never takes delight in multitudes who only have a superficial interest in him. In fact, Jesus subjects those who desire to follow him to the most severe sifting process by making tremendous demands. Many in the crowds were simply curious about him. They wanted to see this new miracle worker. They watched from a distance, however, avoiding real commitment to the Christ.

Jesus teaches that all who wish to follow him must choose him unconditionally as Lord and Master and must make all other loyalties and ties absolutely subordinate to their loyalty and devotion to Christ. Jesus even says our love for him should be so much greater than our love for family that, comparatively, we are "to hate" our families. Rather than strengthening our family ties, following Christ may cost us our relationship to our family! A Jewish student at Southwestern Seminary related that, as a result of proclaiming Jesus as the Christ, he was considered by his family to be dead.

Following Jesus means being willing to bear our cross, to abandon all selfish and self-seeking ambitions, and to deny ourselves in order that we might serve others. Jesus never espoused the bandwagon theology that is characteristic of much of the church growth movement today. He never said, "Jump on board because it's exciting to follow the crowd." On the contrary, he warned his followers in a manner that can be summarized from the Gospel accounts: "Stop. Count the cost. It's dreadfully expensive to follow me. Make sure you're willing to pay the price. It may cost you friends and family. It will cost you your self-serving ambitions. To follow me, you'll have to put self to death. You'll have to pick up your cross."[9] In

Luke 14:28-33 Jesus says you have to count the cost so as not to be ridiculed like the builder who begins but cannot finish.

Flannery O'Conner said, "What people don't realize is how much religion costs. They think faith is a big electric blanket when, of course, it is the cross." Dietrich Bonhoeffer prophetically declared,

> Cheap grace is the deadly enemy of our church. We are fighting today for costly grace. . . . Cheap grace is the preaching of forgiveness without requiring repentance, baptism without church discipline, Communion without confession, absolution without personal confession. Cheap grace is grace without discipleship. . . . Costly grace is the treasure hidden in the field; for the sake of it a man will gladly go and sell all that he has. It is the pearl of great price to buy which the merchant will sell all his goods. . . . It is the call of Jesus Christ at which the disciple leaves his nets and follows him.[10]

Real church growth must issue a clear call to commitment. It must unapologetically call people to commit their time, their resources, and their whole being to Christ and, thus, to his church. Historic Christianity is more than a feel-good solution to depression and stress. It is more than instruction in fatherhood and more than a support group that helps us deal with our past. It is the radical proclamation that a rabbi of 2,000 years ago is the Messiah, the Holy One of Israel, the Lamb of God who takes away the sins of the world. It is allegiance to the one who went to the cross, knowing that even as we follow him we, too, will suffer.[11] Historic Christianity embodies a theology that unashamedly proclaims the wrath of an angry God upon the sin of humanity.[12] It is a new way of life that prohibits us from lavishly supplying ourselves with the luxuries of Western civilization. Rather, it calls us to be good stewards of all we have because, once we proclaim Jesus as Lord, all that we have is his.

While I, too, am tempted to dilute the message, rush people down the aisle, and make it all easy and entertaining, I have determined that yielding to those temptations is not only a mistake, but also completely contrary to the way Jesus called disciples. He asked Matthew to abandon the tax tables and the sons of Zebedee to leave their nets and their father in the boat. He asked would-be disciples not even to take the time to bury their parents or to set their business affairs in order. He urged the rich young ruler to sell all his possessions and give the proceeds to charitable causes. Jesus demanded unconditional allegiance and commitment. He tested his followers before he allowed them to walk in his footsteps. Unlike Christ's costly call to discipleship, we have made following him too easy.

At a meeting of a group of pastors from megachurches, one pastor explained his "easy join plan." While I was not so much offended by the particulars of the plan once explained, the idea that the church ought to be easy to join was extremely troubling.

In a missions class at Southwestern Seminary an Asian student explained that she was perplexed by the fact it is easier to join American churches than it is to get a bus ticket! She remarked that in her country, it means something to be a member of a church; people think seriously before they promise allegiance to a body of believers.

On another occasion a Mennonite pastor was painting during a renovation project at Meadowbrook Baptist Church. The Monday preceding Easter I commented to him as he painted, "I guess you'll be excited about this Sunday—you'll have a large attendance!" My ignorance caused me great embarrassment. The Mennonite pastor had a sincerely puzzled look on his face that I remember to this day. He inquired in all innocence, "Why would we have more worshippers on Easter than we have on any other Sunday? Our members are in church every Sunday unless they are deathly ill." I mumbled, "Well, there shouldn't be any reason, should there?"

lowered my head, and walked away. In that Mennonite community it meant something to follow Christ, to be part of the church. The members had counted the cost, and they were present every single week.

The new, diluted form of evangelicalism reminds me of the story about Jerry. His father had been out of work for nearly four months, and although he didn't know the details of the family finances, nine-year-old Jerry knew things were tight. When his friends talked about a circus coming to town, his first question was, "How much will it cost?" "Five dollars," one friend answered. For days Jerry and his friends wondered and talked about what the circus would be like. It was the main topic of conversation at recess and at lunch.

One day a friend of Jerry's said he had seen a poster about the circus near Wal-Mart. After school they walked the long way home so they could gaze at the poster. It announced "An Old-Fashioned Circus under the Big Top!" The artwork gave promise of spectacular entertainment. The boys had seen every imaginable acrobat and animal act on television, but to see it live and up close was an exciting possibility. None of the boys could remember anything like this ever happening in their little town.

That night after dinner Jerry got up enough courage to ask, "Dad, have you heard about the circus that is coming to town?" "Yes," smiled his father. "Do you think I can go when it comes to town? It's five dollars, and I know that's a lot of money, and I know you've been out of work, and I . . ." Sensing his son's concern, the father interrupted, "I'll tell you what; for the next few days I'm going to help Joe Martin paint his house. After school you come over there, give us a hand, and I'm sure we can scrape up the five dollars."

For the next several afternoons Jerry went straight from school to the Martin home. He scraped boards, ran errands, and generally helped out. By the following Friday news of the circus was everywhere. Frequent announcements were aired on the radio, and the Sunday paper devoted a large section to the circus. Jerry read it over and over.

The final days before the circus seemed to drag on forever. Finally, on Friday evening, Jerry's dad gave him the five dollar bill. Jerry could hardly go to sleep that night, but he was up early Saturday morning. He grabbed a quick breakfast and ran all the way to town. He picked out a prime spot on the curb in front of Crawford's Shoe Store. Then he waited. By ten o'clock the sidewalks had begun to fill up. People jostled Jerry, but he managed to keep his spot. Everyone was ecstatic. The atmosphere was electric.

In the distance, music and the roaring of people could be heard. The sounds grew louder and louder. Jerry shouted when he saw the first clown driving around in circles on a tiny little motorcycle and throwing pieces of candy to children. The clowns were closely followed by elephants, camels, caged lions and tigers, two jugglers, horses ridden by women in beautiful costumes, and a marching band. A float featuring a fat lady and a tall, thin man was followed by a dozen more clowns. The antics of the clowns were so funny that Jerry laughed until tears came to his eyes.

Jerry stood there and took it all in. Sometimes he laughed; other times he was speechless. He had never seen anything like it. As the last clown passed by, Jerry stepped from the curb and handed the five dollar bill to the clown. Then Jerry happily turned and walked toward home. As he passed by Mr. Martin's house, Jerry ran over to his dad and excitedly began to report the events. He described in great detail the various things he had seen. As Jerry finished his story, his father smiled curiously, walked over to Jerry, put his arm around him, and said, "Son, you went to see the circus, but you only saw the parade."[13]

Every Sunday morning people show up at church as spectators and then go home. They think they've seen the church —the community of faith made up of called-out believers—

but, in reality, the only thing they've seen is the parade. The church is made up of a group of people who have counted the cost and followed Christ. Day by day they minister in his name.

Encounter a holy God.

Much of lite church and contemporary worship has ceased to be a God encounter as described in Isaiah 6—the vision of the Lord sitting on a throne, high and lifted up, with the train of His robe filling the Temple. All the symbols together, the title "Lord," the throne, the lofty position, and the all-encompassing robe reinforce the sovereignty of God over the universe. His holiness is extolled by the seraphim in their antiphonal chorus, "Holy, holy, holy."[14]

Many Christians fear that the church of the late twentieth century is becoming so emotional and experiential that we are beginning to lose the formative and the substantive. We have made the experience of church so much like our culture that we are losing our identity as the unique people of God. We must be careful not to cultivate a shallow generation of Christians who need a pep rally to be entertained, a generation whose theology is best summarized on bumper stickers and T-shirts. Even while striving for church growth, we must be careful not to permeate the worship of God with so much adolescent theology that we're all too willing to sacrifice quality for quantity.

The dumbing down of the church is simply a reflection of a process occurring throughout society. In the educational field there are many testimonies to the dumbing down of requirements, the moving away from the formative in education to the experiential. Several years ago Jane Healy, a trainer of educators, wrote a lengthy book entitled *Endangered Minds: Why Our Children Don't Think*. The book grew out of the question she was hearing over and over again from teachers: "Are we less capable, or are our kids actually dumber than they have been in the past?" Healy gives many vivid descriptions of how the educational system has been dumbed down. She shows the difference between a fourth grade reading test from 1964 and an advanced reading test for ninth graders in 1988. The advanced ninth grade test from 1988 is shockingly easier than the fourth grade test from 1964.[15] This is not the teacher's fault. It is not even the administration's fault. The forces of society and culture have created an educational system that has made things easy, simple, and entertaining for our children.

This process happens in church whenever worship planners prioritize drawing a crowd or creating "feel good" experiences.[16] The pattern of worship in Isaiah 6 includes not only the holiness of God, but also the sinfulness of humanity. When Isaiah saw God as He really was—holy, high, and exalted—he also saw himself for who he really was—a sinner in need of forgiveness. When he saw the holiness of God, his worship moved from being a celebration to a confrontation. He was overwhelmed by the sight of his own sinfulness, declaring, "I am a man of unclean lips!" Isaiah gives us the model. When we go to church, our worship should not focus primarily on our own needs, but rather upon the character of God. When we see the holiness of God, we should suffer anguish for our sin.

Hugh Kerr and John Mulder have written a book entitled *Conversions* in which they cite the verbatim testimonies of spiritual leaders from the apostle Paul to Charles Colson, including notables such as Augustine, John Calvin, John Bunyan, John and Charles Wesley, Charles Spurgeon, Leo Tolstoy, William Booth, Albert Schweitzer, C. S. Lewis, and Thomas Merton. Using Isaiah's vision of God as a model, the authors state that in every conversion they studied there was an agony of the soul, the stab of the conscience, the shame of inward uncleanliness, the remorse for sin, and the sensation of being lost and alone. For example, when John Bunyan received a glimpse of the holiness of God, he reported that he felt like a child falling into a mill-pit. Sprawled in water at the bottom of the pit, he could find no handhold or foothold to lift himself out. He felt he would die in the pit. From that memory came the allegory of *Pilgrim's Progress*.[17] When would-be disciples realize their sinfulness, they declare with Isaiah, "Woe is me, for I am undone!"

The worship experience involves not only seeing the holiness of God and the sinfulness of humanity, but also being ready to serve. In Isaiah 6:8-9 the prophet, after seeing God and then seeing himself as a sinner, experiences the forgiveness of God and is ready to serve. "Here am I, Lord. Send me," the prophet declares.

Conclusion

In Soulac, France, a farmer struck his foot on an object in one of his fields. It was the tip of a metal bar protruding out of the ground. He could not imagine who would have driven a stake into his field, but taking his shovel, he tried to dig it out. After digging down about six feet, he realized the task was beyond what he could tackle. Officials from the village, after investigating the situation, brought large, road-building equipment to the site. After two days the workers had sunk a hole more than twenty feet deep. They determined that the "stake" in the field was, in fact, the top of a steeple. Across the centuries dirt, debris, war, and weather had buried an ancient and forgotten church building. Over a period of many months the building was completely uncovered and carefully restored. If you visit Soulac today and ask a taxi driver to drive you to the Verte Ferme chapel, you can stand in a church building that was once buried for more than 800 years.[18]

Think of the community of faith that once occupied Verte Ferme chapel. What had so preoccupied their time and attention that they forgot their church? A great deal of dirt and debris threatens to cover up and bury the church today, especially the community of faith that fails to issue a clear call to commitment. The church can no longer have a "come when you can, we understand" complacent attitude. When we go to church, we need to go for the right reasons—to experience God in His holiness, to see ourselves as sinners in need of forgiveness, and to devote ourselves to service.

People must hear the call of discipleship, take ownership in their church, and be ready and willing to serve. Josh Hunt, at a Sunday School conference in Houston, Texas, asked the participants, "Can you remember the last time you washed a rental car? Probably not. People don't wash rental cars. The motivation of ownership is missing. The same principle is true in churches. Until people feel a degree of ownership, they are going to treat the church like they treat a rented car."[19]

In contrast to this flippant attitude that promotes lite church is the following poem by Edgar A. Guest. The poem was found by Bill Fomby, business administrator at First Baptist Church of Amarillo, in the Bible belonging to his deceased grandmother, Cora Battle Fomby. She understood a costly call to discipleship.

My Church

My Church is the home of my soul, the altar of my devotion, the heart of my faith, the center of my affection, and the foretaste of heaven.

It claims the first place in my activities; and its unity, peace, and progress concern my life in this world and that which is to come. I owe it my zeal, my benevolence, and my prayers.

When I neglect its services I injure its good name, I lessen its power, I discourage its members, I chill my own soul, and disown my allegiance to its founder, the Lord, Jesus Christ.[20]

Churches that are going to grow with integrity must issue a clear call to commitment—no apology.

Notes

[1]During a telephone conversation on 9 October 1998, Ford explained that he felt as though the "mini-service" was successful in reaching new prospects. He did report, however, that those who were attracted to the compact service did not become involved in the church's various ministries and activities. Ford never felt as though his "mini methodology" was compromising the gospel.

[2]Randall O'Brien, *I Feel Better All Over Than I Do Anywhere Else* (Macon GA: Smyth & Helwys, 1999) 53.

[3]This church lite emphasis in some fundamentalist congregations has created the unforeseen scenario by which moderate/conservative churches have now become the bastions of evangelical theology!

[4]Emphasis added.

[5]William Willimon saw an advertisement entitled, "Cappuccino and Christ." Under a coffee mug the ad read: "Sleep a little later, throw on some jeans, have a cup of Joe, listen to some great music, and get together for some wonderful fellowship. _____ Church invites you to join us for a unique service that offers an alternative. No pressures, no commitments, no hassle. All we ask is that you give us forty-five minutes of your Sunday." William H. Willimon, "How 'User-Friendly Churches' Get Used," in *The Library of Distinctive Sermons*, vol. 3, ed. Gary W. Klingsporn (Sisters OR: Questar Publishers, 1996) 129.

[6]I am personal friends with the pastors of both of these congregations that have marketed church lite. Ironically, I think they have falsely described their services, which actually convey a call to discipleship. I object to their description of their worship more than their worship itself.

[7]Marva J. Dawn, *Reaching Out Without Dumbing Down* (Grand Rapids: Eerdmans, 1995) 42.

[8]William H. Willimon, *The Bible: A Sustaining Presence in Worship* (Valley Forge PA: Judson Press, 1981) 33.

[9]Compare to ideas in Matt 8:32-39; 16:24-27.

[10]Dietrich Bonhoeffer, *The Cost of Discipleship* (New York: MacMillan, 1963) 45-48.

[11]2 Tim 3:12; Acts 14:22; Matt 24:9, 21-22. Walter Brueggemann is concerned that a steady diet of upbeat praise music is in direct denial of the many psalms that are songs of lament, protest, and complaint about the incoherence that is experienced in the world. He writes, "At least it is clear that a church that goes on singing 'happy songs' in face of the raw reality is doing something very different from what the Bible itself does." Walter Brueggemann, *The Message of the Psalms: A Theological Commentary*, Augsburg Old Testament Series (Minneapolis: Augsburg, 1984) 51-52.

[12]What will we do with Jonathan Edwards' sermon, "Sinners in the Hands of an Angry God," today?

[13]N. D. Plummer, "A True Story," *Illustration Digest* (December-February 1992/3): 1-2.

[14]David McKenna, *Isaiah 1-39*, Mastering the Old Testament (Dallas: Word Publishing, 1994): 108.

[15]Jane M. Healy, *Endangered Minds: Why Our Children Don't Think* (New York: Simon and Schuster, 1990) 29.

[16]Dallas Willard compares the contemporary "feel good" approach to life to Paul's world that took for granted the disciplines for spiritual life. He wrote, "Thoughtful and religiously devout people of the classical and Hellenistic world, from the Ganges to the Tiber, knew that the mind and body of the human being had to be rigorously disciplined to achieve a decent individual and social existence. This is not something St. Paul had to prove or even explicitly state to his readers—but it also was not something that he overlooked, leaving it to be brought up by crazed monks in the Dark Ages." Willard argues that our idea about "doing what feels good" finds its roots in the eighteenth-century idealization of happiness as it is filtered through the nineteenth-century English ideology of pleasure as "the good" for people. Willard regrets that our present method of measuring the success of a worship service based upon whether people "feel good" is a result of adopting popular culture in popular religion. See Dallas Willard, *The Spirit of the Disciplines* (San Francisco: HarperCollins, 1991) 99.

[17]Hugh Kerr and John Mulder, eds., *Conversions: The Christian Experience* (Grand Rapids: Eerdmans, 1983) 48-53. Compare also the early African experience in America as reported in Barbara Brown Zikmund, ed., *God Struck Me Dead: Voices of Ex-Slaves* (Cleveland OH: Pilgrim Press, 1993) 59. Like all other conversions, the African experience included Isaiah's agony of the soul. One slave said his conversion experience was as if "God struck me dead with his power!" In his vision he saw hell and the

devil as he crawled along a brick wall, trying not to fall in a dark, roaring pit.

[18]*Illustration Digest* (November/December/January 1994/5): 2.

[19]Josh Hunt, "Small Group Ministry Through the Sunday School," Innovative Church Growth Conference, Houston TX, January 1994

[20]Unable to verify the author as Edgar A. Guest or find the poem among his collections of poetry.

Treat everyone as a valued person.

When new families move to town, they often visit numerous churches, looking for the place where they "fit in." What factors contribute to a positive first experience? What factors contribute to visitors "feeling at home" in your church? How do we relate to people in a manner that creates a favorable first impression? The answer is really very simple. Treat people in the same way you want to be treated. Embody the same characteristics you admire in others.

Be genuine.

Nothing turns people away more quickly than insincerity. Knuckle-cracking handshakes, backslaps, and forced booming voices all combine to establish the aura of a used car lot. Be natural. Be genuine. Be yourself. Any element in the visitor's experience that establishes you as a commissioned salesperson and them as a potential buyer leaves a negative impression. If we have our script memorized and simply fill in the blanks with different names, we create a very cold, commercial atmosphere.

A physician in our church recently visited a congregation in another part of the state. "What was your experience?" I probed. "Well, the pastor is really good—but a little too slick." The difference between sincerity and "slickness" is the difference between a basket of delicious Granny Smith apples and a basket of blemish-free, polished, plastic fruit. Real apples are inviting; fake fruit gathers dust. Just as you are attracted to people and places that seem genuine, visitors to your church will be attracted by the same warm atmosphere.

Remember names.

Nothing holds more power than a name. Biblical examples of "name power" are too numerous to survey comprehensively. During Jacob's struggle with the angel in Genesis 32, each wrestler asked the other his name. By giving his name, Jacob had to confess his nature—a crafty over-reacher, a heel-catcher. He had to identify his true nature—Jacob—before he could be blessed—Israel. The divine assailant, on the contrary, refused to reveal his name because he didn't want Jacob to exercise power over him. His divine name could not be had on demand or taken in vain, lest it be exposed to magical manipulation. Jacob had to be content with a visitation from a "man" whom he realized was divine.[1]

Judges 13 gives another example of name power in the story of Manoah and his barren wife. The angel of the Lord appeared to Manoah's wife and said, "Behold, you are barren and have born no children, but you shall conceive and give birth to a son" (v. 3). The angel instructed her carefully to avoid any strong drink or unclean food and to ensure that no razor ever touched the boy's head because he was to be a Nazarite to God—even from the womb. Missing the divine messenger's visit, Manoah was unsettled and prayed that God would send the messenger once again. On the angel's return visit Manoah convinced him to stay for dinner, but the angel refused to partake of any food. Rather, he wanted to see it prepared as an offering to the Lord. Manoah asked the divine messenger, "What is your name?" (v. 17). The angel of the Lord said to him, "Why do you ask my name, seeing it is wonderful?" (v. 18). The divine messenger of the Lord was then caught up in the flame and smoke that ascended to heaven. Astonished, Manoah and his wife bowed in reverence, knowing they were in the presence of the angel of the Lord.

To know someone's name is to yield influence in his life. What was true in the days of the Old Testament is true today. You cannot begin to know me until you first know my name. In order to be successful leaders in a congregation, the pastor and staff must make every effort to learn as many names as possible. People feel as if you respect and honor them if you have taken the time to learn their names. Of course, this is no easy task. In some very large congregations, it is absolutely impossible. Nonetheless, learning names should still be a priority even if the task will never be completed.

After having been introduced to someone, we often cannot recall her name even minutes later because we were focusing on what type of impression we were making. The greatest key to learning names is to relax. Focus on the other person when her name is being given, and then immediately repeat her name. "Pastor, I'd like for you to meet Sarah Duckingham. She's new in town. She teaches first grade at Clear Creek Elementary. She moved into an apartment right beside mine." In order to learn her name, look Sarah eye to eye and repeat her name, making certain that you have correctly understood: "Sarah Duckingham. Sarah, we're sure glad you're here to visit with us today." In order to remember names, listen to the other person and focus on her rather than on yourself.

Convey interest in others.

Have you ever contemplated what you really like in other people? Why does someone stand out as exceptional among a group of friends? Often the people we feel fond of have shown an interest in us. How long do you like to be around people who talk about "me, myself, and I," people who are always topping your last story, people who play a game of one-upmanship, or people who see all of life as a competition?

When a self-centered egomaniac enters a room, we throw up our defenses, become tense, and retreat. If you want to be able to form relationships quickly and attract people to your congregation, then you must be a person who is willing to focus on others and listen with undivided attention in a way that communicates you genuinely care.

Mrs. Leonard, a second-grade school teacher, had the rare gift of communicating her sincere interest in others. Her concern for others was life changing for Mary Ann Bird. Mary Ann remembers:

> I grew up knowing I was different, and I hated it. I was born with a cleft palate, and when I started school, my classmates made it clear to me how I looked to others: a little girl with a misshapen lip, crooked nose, lopsided teeth, and garbled speech.
>
> When schoolmates asked, "What happened to your lip?" I'd tell them I'd fallen and cut it on a piece of glass. Somehow it seemed more acceptable to have suffered an accident than to have been born different. I was convinced that no one outside my family could love me.
>
> There was, however, a teacher in the second grade whom we all adored—Mrs. Leonard. She was short, round, happy—a sparkling lady.
>
> Annually we had a hearing test. . . . Mrs. Leonard gave the test to everyone in the class, and finally it was my turn. I knew from past years that as we stood against the door and covered one ear, the teacher sitting at her desk would whisper something, and we would have to repeat it back— things like, "The sky is blue" or "Do you have new shoes?" I waited there for those words that God must have put into her mouth, those seven words that changed my life. Mrs. Leonard said, in her whisper, "I wish you were my little girl."[2]

Avoid showing favoritism.

Many churches have tension between factions because the pastor identifies with only one segment of the congregation. The favoritism might be caused by a theological identification with the conservatives or moderates or by a generational identification with young couples or senior adults. The partiality might be toward a particular demographic profile as the pastor only focuses on families who live in a certain part of town or who have power and influence in the community.

To be like Christ, a pastor must treat everyone equally and fairly. If the cry of the prophet for protection for the widow and orphan means anything in the Old Testament, and if the teachings of Jesus mean anything in the New Testament, then we must treat each one as a valued person. The very essence of the Kingdom of God demands that all prejudicial judgments be turned upside down. Those who suppose themselves to be great are humbled, and those who are humbled become great.

James insists that we show no partiality. "My brethren," wrote the brother of Jesus, "do not hold your faith in our glorious Lord Jesus Christ with the attitude of personal favoritism." When church leaders understand the necessity of treating everyone equally, then the church becomes the one place on earth where the standards of the world are cast aside. When we come to church, we should not be judged by our wealth,[3] intelligence, social standing, beauty,[4] or any other category established by sinful humanity. Rather, church should be the one place where people are treated equally at the foot of the cross.

James teaches us that if someone comes into the church wearing a gold ring and fine clothes and another arrives with shabby clothes, we should not pay special attention to the one who is wearing the fine clothes by saying, "Hey, we've saved a great seat for you on the front row," while we say to the poor person, "You sit on the floor." If we play favorites, we have made distinctions among ourselves and become "judges with evil motives." James exhorts, "Listen my brethren, did not God choose the poor of this world to be rich in faith and heirs of the kingdom which He promised to those who love Him?" (2:1-5).[5] James' call to accept everyone was put to the test, however, the day Bill came to church!

Bill has wild hair, and his entire wardrobe consists of T-shirts with holes, well-worn jeans, and bare feet—no shoes. He is philosophical, esoteric, and very bright. During his tenure in college Bill proclaimed the Lordship of Jesus Christ, accepting him as Savior.

Located directly across the street from the university Bill attends is a well-dressed, traditional congregation. Because of the church's location, the members really want to begin a ministry to university students, but they are not sure how to go about it.

One day, because of his new faith, Bill decides to go to the church. Arriving late, he has to meander down the aisle to look for an available seat. The church is packed, and he cannot find an open space on the pews.

Drawing closer and closer to the pulpit and realizing there are no seats, he simply squats down Indian-style on the carpet. While this is perfectly acceptable behavior for a college fellowship, no one has ever sat in the floor of this church before! By now, the people are really uptight, and tension pervades the service.

As Bill creates his own place, the pastor spies an elderly deacon making his way from the back of the church toward Bill. If Bill's wild hair, T-shirt, jeans, and bare feet make him stand out in this traditional congregation, this eighty-year-old deacon blends in perfectly with the elderly congregation— silver hair, a three-piece suit, and a pocket watch. His whole demeanor is distinguished and dignified. Rebecca Manley Pippert concludes the story:

He walks with a cane, and as he starts walking toward this boy, everyone is saying to themselves, *You can't blame him for what he's going to do. How can you expect a man of his age and of his background to understand some college kid on the floor?*

It takes a long time for the man to reach the boy. The church is utterly silent except for the clicking of the man's cane. All eyes are focused on him; you can't even hear anyone breathing. The people are thinking, *The minister can't even preach the sermon until the deacon does what he has to do.*

And now they see this elderly man drop his cane on the floor. With great difficulty, he lowers himself and sits down next to Bill and worships with him so he won't be alone. Everyone chokes up with the emotion. When the minister gains control he says, "What I'm about to preach, you will never remember. What you have just seen, you will never forget."[6]

If we are to be part of the Kingdom of God, we cannot judge according to the standards of the world.

Treating all people as valued individuals means seeing them as God sees them rather than merely looking at their wealth or beauty. Part of the story of ancient Israel is the story of selecting a king. Like all its neighboring nations, ancient Israel wanted a monarchy instead of a theocracy in which God sits on the throne. In 1 Samuel 8 God says, "They have rejected me from being king over them" (v. 7). God warns that having a king is not pleasing to Him and will have unpleasant results for the Israelites. God cautions them that a king will take their daughters for perfumers, cooks, and bakers; the best of their fields; their male servants; and a tenth of their flocks. They will be in slavery to a human king. The people, however, shout out, "There shall be a king over us" (v. 19), and God relents.

In the account of the selection of the first king, Saul is described as a handsome man: "There was not a more handsome man than he among all the sons of Israel. From his shoulders up, he was taller than any of the people" (9:2; 10:23-24). Saul's reign, however, inaugurates a subtheme woven into the entire narrative of Samuel: a handsome leader does evil in the sight of the Lord.

In 2 Samuel 14 another handsome character, Absalom, the son of David, conspires against his own father. Remember how Absalom is described? "Now in all Israel there was no one as handsome as Absalom, so highly praised from the soul of his foot to the crown of his head there was no defect in him" (v. 25). Absalom is a handsome man, qualified to adorn the cover of *GQ*. He is perfect from head to toe, yet he is rejected by God.

When the handsome King Saul is being replaced, the Lord tells Samuel he will choose one of the sons of the Bethlehemite Jesse as the new king. He has Samuel invite Jesse and his boys to attend a sacrifice. When the oldest son of Jesse, Eliab, comes forward, Samuel—remembering how tall and handsome Saul is—thinks to himself, "Surely the Lord's anointed is before me." The Lord, however, says to Samuel: "Don't look at his appearance or the height of his stature because I have rejected him. For God sees not as a man sees, for man looks at the outward appearance, but the Lord looks at the heart" (2 Sam 16:6). God chooses David, the youngest, the least of the brothers of Jesse, to become king because God looks at the heart.

The narrative demonstrates that a handsome king is not necessarily a godly king. When it comes time to choose the second king for ancient Israel, beauty will no longer be the criterion. God says, "I don't judge people like you judge people, Samuel!"

Our society has made superficial criteria such as physical attractiveness the basis for judging character. Frederick Buechner concluded,

> To be born as blond and blue-eyed and beautiful as my mother was can be as much a handicap in its own way as to be born with a cleft palate because if you are beautiful enough, you don't really have to be anything much else to make people love you and want to be near you. You don't have to be particularly kind or unselfish or generous or compassionate because people will flock around you anyway simply for the sake of your beauty.[7]

God turns our criteria upside down. God calls upon us to treat all people as valuable and to stop playing our games of favoritism based upon beauty, wealth, and power. To be like God is to treat each person as a valued person.

Ben Burton learned the importance of valuing everyone. In a story he contributed to *A 2nd Helping of Chicken Soup for the Soul*,[8] he tells of a childhood sin of discrimination that has haunted him for years. He remembers:

> Andy was a sweet, amusing little guy whom everyone liked but harassed, just because that was the way one treated Andy Drake. He took the kidding well. He always smiled back with those great big eyes that seemed to say, "Thank you, thank you, thank you," with each sweeping blink.
>
> For us fifth-graders, Andy was our outlet; he was our whipping boy. He even seemed grateful to pay this special price for membership in our group.
>
> *Andy Drake don't eat no cake,*
> *And his sister don't eat no pie.*
> *If it wasn't for the welfare dole,*
> *All the Drakes would die.*

Andy even appeared to like this sing-song parody of Jack Spratt. The rest of us really enjoyed it, bad grammar and all.

I don't know why Andy had to endure this special treatment to deserve our friendship and membership in the group. It just evolved naturally—no vote or discussion.

Andy's father was in prison, and his mother was so busy entertaining men that she did little to teach her son personal hygiene—rusty elbows and dirty fingernails. He wore a coat that was two sizes too big. Despite the verbal attacks from the other boys, Andy never fought back. While the boys all felt superior to Andy, they, nonetheless, liked him in an odd sort of way. They liked him, that is, until one of them insisted that because Andy was so different, they didn't want him to be part of "their group" any longer. Burton explains:

"He's different! We don't want him, do we?"

Which one of us said it? I've wanted to blame Randolph all these years, but I can't honestly say who spoke those trigger words that brought out the savagery lying dormant but so near the surface in all of us. It doesn't matter who, for the fervor with which we took up the cry revealed us all.

"I didn't want to do what we did."

For years I tried to console myself with that. Then one day I stumbled on those unwelcome but irrefutable words that convicted me forever:

The hottest corners of hell are reserved for those who, during a moment of crisis, maintain their neutrality.

Often, after the Friday bell rang and school was out for the weekend, the boys met at one of the homes of the members of "the group." This particular Friday, Ben's house was the gathering place for a camp-out. The mothers prepared for these childhood "safaris"; they even fixed an extra pack for Andy who was going to join the others after doing his chores. Groups can often provide a seedbed for cruel courage. Because they were at his house, the other boys elected Ben to kick Andy out of the group. Ben Burton protests:

> Me? I who had long believed that Andy secretly thought a little more of me than he did the others because of the puppy-like way he looked at me? I who often felt him revealing his love and appreciation with those huge, wide-open eyes?
>
> I can still plainly see Andy as he came toward me down the long, dark tunnel of trees that leaked only enough of the late afternoon light to kaleidoscope changing patterns on his soiled old sweatshirt. Andy was on his rusty, one-of-a-kind bike—a girl's model with sections of garden hose wired to the rims for tires. He appeared excited and happier than I had ever seen him, this frail little guy who had been an adult all of his life. I knew he was savoring the acceptance by the group, this first chance to belong, to have "boy fun," to do "boy things."

Andy waved as Ben stood nervously waiting to accomplish his dirty deed. Andy's spirit was filled with the jubilation expected of a young lad who had been released from the confinement of the school house into the freedom of the woods. As Andy chattered gleefully, the other boys remained concealed within the tent, yet showing their silent support for Ben, the messenger of grim news.

Ben could only hope that Andy would realize his gaiety was not being reciprocated. Andy's joyful babbling only made giving him the boot all the more difficult. At last, Andy realized that he was about to be the victim of cruel, childhood arrogance:

His whole demeanor said, "It's going to be very bad, isn't it, Ben? Let's have it." Undoubtedly well-practiced in facing disappointment, he didn't even brace for the blow. Andy never fought back.

Incredulously, I heard myself say, "Andy, we don't want you."

Hauntingly vivid still is the stunning quickness with which two huge tears sprang into Andy's eyes and just stayed there. Vivid because of a million maddening reruns of that scene in my mind. The way Andy looked at me—frozen for an eternal moment—what was it? It wasn't hate. Was it shock? Was it disbelief? Or, was it pity—for me?

Or forgiveness?

Finally, a fleet little tremor broke across Andy's lips, and he turned without appeal, or even a question, to make the long, lonely trip home in the dark.

After the dirty deed was done, a silence fell over the now-elite gang. The graveness of the moment began to sink in as they pondered their own cruelty. They heard Jesus' words for the first time with understanding, "Inasmuch as you do it unto the least of these." By their rejection, they had destroyed one made in the image of the Creator.

Because his school attendance was erratic, no one knew when Andy actually withdrew from school. Ben was so self-focused that he never took the time to apologize to Andy. In fact, he never saw Andy again. But he has long been haunted by his cruel deed. He explains,

> In the decades since that autumn day in the Arkansas woods, I have encountered thousands of Andy Drakes. My conscience places Andy's mask over the face of every disadvantaged person with whom I come in contact. Each one stares back at me with that same haunting, expectant look that became fixed in my mind that day long ago.

Ben Burton concludes his story with this letter to Andy:

Dear Andy Drake:

The chance you will ever see these words is quite remote, but I must try. It's much too late for this confession to purge my conscience of guilt. I neither expect it to nor want it to.

What I do pray for, my little friend of long ago, is that you might somehow learn of and be lifted by the continuing force of your sacrifice. What you suffered at my hands that day and the loving courage you showed, God has twisted, turned, and molded into a blessing. This knowledge might ease the memory of that terrible day for you.

I've been no saint, Andy, nor have I done all the things I could and should have done with my life. But what I want you to know is that I have never again knowingly betrayed an Andy Drake. Nor, I pray, shall I ever.

Ben Burton

Notes

[1]Allen P. Ross, *Creation and Blessing: A Guide to the Study and Exposition of Genesis* (Grand Rapids: Baker Book House, 1988) 546-59.

[2]Edward K. Rowell, ed., *Fresh Illustrations for Preaching and Teaching* (Grand Rapids: Baker Books, 1997) 8.

[3]Former President Jimmy Carter has said, "Most church members—including me—rarely reach out to people who are different from us or less fortunate. Quite often my Sunday school class will say, 'Why don't we take up a collection and give a nice Thanksgiving meal to a poor family?' The next question is: 'Who knows a poor family?' Nobody does. We have to call the welfare office." *Christian Reader* 35/4 (July/Aug 1997): 29.

[4]In a series of groundbreaking experiments, psychologist Judith Langlois of the University of Texas, Austin, has shown that even infants share a sense of what is attractive. In the late 1980s Langlois started placing 3- and 6-month-old babies in front of a screen and showing them pairs of facial photographs. Each pair included one considered attractive by adult judges and one considered unattractive. In the first study, she found that the infants gazed significantly longer at "attractive" white female faces than at "unattractive" ones. Since then, she has repeated the drill using

white male faces, black female faces, and even the faces of other babies; the same pattern always emerges. "These kids don't read *Vogue* or watch TV," Langlois says. "They haven't been touched by the media. Yet they make the same judgments as adults." Geoffrey Crowley, "The Biology of Beauty," *Newsweek* 127/23 (3 June 1996): 62-63.

[5]Dallas Willard wrote, "Only if we believe with our whole being in the equality of rich and poor before God can we walk in their midst as Jesus did, unaffected in our personal relations by the distinction." Dallas Willard, *The Spirit of the Disciplines* (San Francisco: HarperCollins, 1991) 209.

[6]Rebecca Manley Pippert, "A Guy Named Bill," in *More Stories for the Heart*, edited by Alice Gray (Sisters, OR: Multnomah Publishers, 1997) 32-33. Punctuation is from original story.

[7]Frederick Buechner, *Telling Secrets* (New York: HarperSanFrancisco, 1991) 15.

[8]Ben Burton, "The Martyrdom of Andy." In *A 2nd Helping of Chicken Soup for the Soul*, compiled by Jack Canfield and Mark Victor Hansen (Deerfield Beach FL: Health Communications, Inc., 1995) 50-54.

Conclusion

A couple had been married for fifty years. Their friends and family gave them a golden wedding anniversary reception. Being moved by the evening's events, the old man stood to offer a word of appreciation to his wife of half a century. He said, "When we married, neither of us was sure how it would turn out. But through the years you have proven yourself tried and true." She was a bit hard of hearing, so she asked, "What did you say?" He repeated a bit louder, "You've proven yourself tried and true." Again she cried out, "What?" "I said," he responded still louder, "you are tried and true." At that she yelled back, "Oh yeah, well I'm tired of you, too!"

In this book I have shared ten principles for effective ministry. They all have one thing in common: Each principle was derived from listening to the congregation and prospects of the congregation. Ironically, seminary professors spend a great deal of time teaching ministers to talk. Each student's preaching is graded on inflection, grammar, pronunciation, dynamics, and body language, along with a host of other intangible qualities. While this is a needed discipline, perhaps we would do well to have a lesson on listening. Effective ministry is much more dependent on excellent listening skills than excellent speaking skills. Every minister must seek to discover the central voice of his people.

A few years ago Paine-Webber conducted a marketing campaign that emphasized the company's ability to listen to its clients' needs and, therefore, custom-design an investment portfolio for each individual investor. Perhaps you remember the ads: "How did your broker know you wanted to retire early?" "He asked."[1]

The campaign peddled the idea that Paine-Webber representatives actually listen to their clients. Perhaps the ability to listen is so rare in major corporations that Paine-Webber thought they could market listening as a commodity.

How does this approach compare to the E. F. Hutton slogan: "When E. F. Hutton talks, people listen." The E. F. Hutton campaign failed—the company went out of business. Paine-Webber, however, is still handling accounts because the public was convinced their brokers were listening. People don't want investors who tell them what to do; rather, they want investors who listen to their needs, hopes, and dreams. What is true of stockbrokers is also true of ministers. People want a minister who listens.

Each of these ten principles of church growth is built on the foundation of listening carefully to the congregation. Only a listening pastor can build a healthy pastoral ministry. In fact, as I ponder my activities from day to day, I listen so much that it is actually exhausting. In the hallways, in the grocery store, wherever I am, people want to share their frustrations, joys, and sorrows. People want to be heard.

Building an exemplary staff can take place only if we are careful to listen during the interviewing and reference-checking processes, and to listen to what other search committee members say about possible staff members. We can only form programs that meet needs if we have first discovered those needs by listening. Whether we are trying to create positive self-esteem in a congregation or recognize children and youth as decision makers, we must develop listening skills. These ten principles issue a call for ministers to listen patiently and with understanding in order to establish healthy congregations.

Hugh Downs tells a great story about listening. Years ago, when he was working in radio, he watched an experienced colleague interview a man who had escaped from a Kremlin prison. The man told how it had taken him months to tunnel out. He dug and dug and ate the dirt around him. When he figured that his tunnel was outside the prison walls, he began digging upward, trying to reach the surface. One midnight he was finally ready to break through. He tunneled through a wooden platform above his head. He then told the interviewer, "When I put my head through the hole, I suddenly realized that I was in the middle of Josef Stalin's office!" The escapee paused, and at that point the interviewer interjected, "So . . . say, do you have any hobbies?" He wasn't listening! This seasoned veteran wasn't paying any attention to the man he was interviewing. Hugh Downs said that watching a colleague's mistake taught him a tremendous lesson about the art of listening.[2] Each of these ten principles requires the minister to be a skilled listener.

Notes

[1]"When the Going Gets Tough," *Sermon Notes and Illustrations* 3/4 (April 1996) 16.

[2] Ibid., 16-17.